I, Alone!

Mastering Life's Seven Principles

Aristides Priakos

I, Alone!
Mastering Life's Seven Principles

Aristides Priakos

Published by: STPG PRESS
San Antonio, TX
Mr. Tim Lippard
tlippard@southtexasprintguy.com

Cover Design & Photo: Sixto Serrano
A special thanks to Ms. Arlena Hutton for her great eyes
and proofing skills.

Copyright © 2015 by Aristides Priakos
ISBN# 9781941174050

All rights reserved

No part of this publication may be reproduced or stored in any manner, without the written consent of the authors; except for brief quotations in critical articles of review.

Printed in the United States of America

References:
- Character Counts in Iowa from the website of the same name; "The Story of the Seed"
- www.openthemeeting.com quote from Abraham Lincoln
- A collection of wisdom through Hindu passages from the Hindu scriptures.
- Jim Rohn-Network Marketing Skills

Table of Contents

Introduction 5

Principle #1 Make Great Decisions 7
    Predict Your Future 9
    Business Buffoonery 20
    Pride and Ego 25

Principle #2 Be Better Tomorrow Than You Were Today 33
    My Painful Memory 35
    Our Own Painful Past 44
    Better Suggestions 51

Principle #3 Be of the Highest of Integrity 55
    Sharing With Others 61
    Your Following 64
    The Seed of Integrity 73

Principle #4 Always Seek Wisdom 77
    The Atom Smasher 77
    Wisdom Is All Truths In the Universe 88
    The Wisdom of Consciousness 92
    The Wisdom In Philosophy 94
    Wisdom of The Universe 98
    Within Lies Wisdom 99

Principle #5 Remove Everything Negative 102
    How Negativity Affects Your Life 103
    How The Brain Processes Negativity 109
    The Emotional Kill Cycle 112

 Your Emotions And Negativity 117

 Breaking the Cycle of Negativity 122

 The Bull's-Eye Targets of 123

 Conflict and Desire 123

Principle #6 Love Yourself First 134

 Your Attitude Is Everything 135

 Your Brain Needs Goals To Love 140

 Self Love and Relationships 142

Principle #7 Serve Others 146

 Serving Unselfishly 148

 The Note From Above 152

 Serving Your Mind 155

 It's The Small Things That Count 160

 Serving The Sick and Special Needs 163

Conclusion and Acknowledgement 169

Introduction

When you read this book, it is my hope that you understand that we must always try to be the masters of our lives. It is a continuing process. Sometimes it is pleasurable, and sometimes it is painful. How you change your direction and your mind-set to apply these principles to make your life more rewarding and fulfilling is the key element that I want you to take from this book.

You can be a master at "mastering" something--but in order to be able to master anything, you must start somewhere. Some never start so they never make nor experience the great and positive outcomes from the much needed changes that are required to make one's life more fulfilling. So how can you attempt to master anything if there is no beginning? Interestingly enough, and the irony as well, is that there is never an end to mastering anything. We should always be seeking and learning.

So, why did I call this book "I, Alone! Mastering Life's Seven Principles?" I named it such because ultimately it is "you" that must take the first step. I don't care what anyone says-- you can have all the support systems in place but it is still "you" that must decide to start somewhere. "Alone" does not mean that you have to go through it or grow alone--it just means that you, alone, must take the first step to positive change.

One such joke describes the above comment. "How many psychiatrists does it take to change a light bulb? Just one, but the light bulb really has to want to change!"

A funny joke, but the meaning holds so very true. You must want to start to change, and the one thing that must change first is your mind-set. You are the only one that can do that.

Taking action stems from our ability to think for ourselves, and the actions and the steps you take will always result in continually making a decision to do something.

Good, bad or indifferent, we make these decisions based purely on thought. Unfortunately, we make it difficult on ourselves, and many people do not take stock and responsibility for their actions. What do you think your results will be if you take zero action? Pretty bleak, isn't it? Thus, any attempt to master anything will fall short of our own expectations if you do not start and take action first.

All of our thoughts, emotions, and logic are tied into one collective stream of consciousness. In order to master anything, the collection of your thoughts and emotions will dictate an action which will then lead you into some type of direction.

Direction is just one element to mastering anything, and the direction and focus you have requires some sort of guidance. It must have constant nurturing, and it must contain one key element that most forget--your ability or process to stay on track and never waiver. That is the tough part, but it is not beyond anyone's ability.

When you finish reading this book, I hope that you reflect on where you are at this point in your life. You must then take some kind of direction and apply all of these principles each and every day of your life. Continuing to do these seven things over and over again will get you some pretty amazing results very quickly.

Principle #1

Make Great Decisions

As I started this chapter, I thought about some of the decisions that I made in my life. I might have changed a few things, but then again, none of us would be where we are at this particular point in time if we changed just one thing in our past. Therein lies the dichotomy—you cannot change anything in your past so why even think about it? Because we are human and we do things like that. Let me ask you a question. If you knew that you could go backwards in time and change just one thing, not knowing the outcome of that action and what it would do to your life in the present, would you do it? I don't think many of us would. Because you just don't know. That "fear" is sometimes what stops us from making "great decisions."

At this point you would start second guessing yourself. "I should have done this, or I should have done that." Many have said to themselves, "If hadn't been so stupid when I was younger, I would not be in the mess that I'm in right now." Easy to say now isn't it? Is it financial? Did you marry too young? Did you marry the wrong person or stay together just for the sake of children? Did you pass up on a job you knew you should have taken? Did you pass on buying Apple when it was 25 cents a share and say to yourself "Aww…computers will never catch on?" Let me clue you in on something. Stop beating yourself up as there is nothing in the world you can do about it. The past is the past, and it is what it is.

Let me give you something to think about for a minute--the decisions you made two, or perhaps five years ago, are indeed affecting your life in the here and now.

That is not my opinion—it is a fact. I think all of us at some point in our lives have possibly second guessed ourselves and said, "If I had a chance to do it over again I would change this or I would change that." Going back to my initial question: If you had a chance to do it all over again, what would you change?

You might change where you live or perhaps you might have done something differently. You would most certainly not be where you are today. Decisions require that you take action, and by taking action, positively or negatively, it will always determine an outcome. Always! If your thought process is of mal intent then your outcome will have negative or even disastrous results. You knew going into the thought process of that decision that the outcome may not be in your favor.

I'll give you an example. A man is at a horse track. He only has $50 left in his pocket. His choices are few, aren't they? Does he take that 50 bucks and bet on a horse that has odds against him, or does he use that money to go home and feed his family? "He has a gambling problem," you might say. He may very well have a gambling problem, but that is not the point here, so stay with me on this.

His thought process requires him to act on that thought at that exact moment in time. That action now requires him to make a decision. If he takes the money and steps up to the window and bets it all on the number five horse, his odds of winning are very low. Yes, he is gambling with that money; but isn't that what many of us do when we make poor decisions? You are gambling with your own outcome-

-your future! The decision that he made betting on that horse will inevitably create an outcome that he knows may potentially have a terrible result.

Think about it for a minute. If you make a decision that you know deep down is the wrong thing to do, you are truly gambling with the outcome of those actions because you have just given up the control of your own destiny. The betting man, in this example, had to make a decision that required action, which most often will result in a negative outcome. Of course, I use the gambling illustration because it is easy to understand and hopefully everyone "gets it." Here is the first nugget of the book—"Every decision that you will ever make for the rest of your life will require you to take some type of action."

This is not that complicated to understand, is it? We make decisions all day, and sometimes we don't even know we are doing it because our subconscious is so strong that we do things by default—like driving, making coffee or even shopping. You know what you have to do when you take action because you have done that same action so many times before. It becomes routine—you are conditioned.

What about the events in your life that have not yet been determined by your decisions? For instance, what about a new job that you are considering, a marriage proposal, or even the decision to have a baby? All of these have not reached an outcome because a decision to "act" has not yet been determined.

Predict Your Future

How do you make a great decision? You must first, and in every case, try to consider the potential outcome. You are almost trying to predict your own future. You may say to yourself, "that sounds ridiculous." However, you can determine many of the variables far in advance of taking action because you should have a keen understanding of the differences between right and wrong. Almost all decisions are based on right and wrong. Period! End of subject! The actions that you take based on your thoughts and decisions will invariably create a positive or negative outcome.

I'm not talking about picking the right or wrong golf club. "Dang, if I hadn't used the seven-iron I'd be on the green right now instead of the sand trap!" No. That is not what I mean. I am merely stating that right and wrong will be based on what you have learned in the past, a social authority, or even God for that matter, and what it is you use as a reference point to direct your thoughts. The ability you possess to utilize your brain to think freely for yourself will help you make the best decision you are capable of making. A great decision is something you should always strive for and seek.

Going back to my earlier question: what benefits will you receive from that new job? How does it affect your life? Will you have to move? Will it require you to take on a great deal more responsibility? Do you feel good about the people that are involved with this potential new position?

What about the case of asking someone to marry you? That is a pretty big decision, isn't it? It is probably one of the biggest decisions you will ever make, next to having a baby, but I will delve into that in just a few minutes. Marriage is not something you jump into as something very important must happen first. You must develop a sense of trust with that other person.

Not only is that person supposed to be your best friend, but now you must consider the fact that both of you must now make great decisions together. That requires a great deal of trust and confidence in the other person's ability to make great decisions on your behalf, as well as theirs. Pretty interesting, isn't it?

Gaining trust from another person does not happen overnight. Just like anything else, it is a process that happens over a period of time. That time period, however it looks for you, must pass and certain things must happen to "earn" that trust, as we like to say in our society. Trust is earned by doing something for another person in little bits and pieces.

Let me give you an example. Would you "trust" someone to watch your child if you only knew them for a few days? Absolutely not! If you did, then that would not be making a great decision, would it? But how did you know so fast the outcome of that decision? Because it is engrained in our subconscious as we know what is right and what is wrong. It would be wrong to trust someone with your child only knowing them for a few days. That is a "trust" that is developed over a period of time. It is something we just know what to do.

Remember, humans are social animals, and we have a structure already in place. We know that a decision, such as the above example illustrates, is so very simple to understand. And we do this time and time again. If you recall a few paragraphs above, I was going to tell you about having a baby. Here is the interesting thing about this. Coming naked into this world (as well as our early childhood) is the ONLY time we have absolutely zero control of making great decisions, or making any decisions at all, for that matter.

We have no control whatsoever where we were born, who are parents are, or what our socio-economic status is. We have no control of our ethnicity, our religion, our creed, the color of our skin or even our gender. What is incredibly amazing about the gender of our children is today we have the medical technology to help define and develop the sex of our children.

I'm sure you now realize why this is so important. The how's, what's and why's of your actions and the decisions that you make, and will make henceforth, will affect the outcome of your future as well as those around you.

This is why we must make great decisions and not just good ones. How do you know if you are making a great decision, you may be asking yourself--ah…well read on my friends as this is where the rubber meets the road, so to speak.

Let's first take a look at some really bad decisions--ones that affected a large number of people all over the world. You don't have to look too far to find them. How about corporate America? The poor decisions that our business leaders made adversely affected hundreds of thousands, if not millions, of people, including countries. Funny thing is that these are the people that we were supposed to "trust."

One great example, of recent times, is the crash and burn of the mortgage and home industry. This was nothing short of making really stupid decisions fueled by selfishness and greed. It wasn't enough that our leaders made really bad decisions with our bond and stock portfolios. Even after the collapse of the markets domestic and abroad, we felt betrayed. The executives that should have gone to jail and did not and made millions and tens of millions of dollars on their golden parachutes. People were wiped out financially all over the world. Some countries went flat broke because of some really, really bad decisions.

I am speaking as an expert here because as a former investment banker and bond trader, I was in the center of all of this nonsense, and I saw it coming many years before it actually happened. Many hundreds of books have been written about the crash that almost mirrored The Great Depression, so I will not elaborate too much on the subject as many of you reading this experienced it first-hand. So, let me share some information with you from someone that was on the "inside" as to these events, and what precipitated these embarrassingly bad decisions. As an author, I am taking creative license in how I describe the following events to you.

I was living in California at the time and managing a very large bond portfolio. I ran the institutional side of the investment business, which means I did not handle retail customers. The retail investment side typically only deals with Mr. and Mrs. John Q. Public. Institutional transactions meant that I was only dealing with cities, municipalities, counties, endowments, trusts and pensions for teachers, firefighters and law enforcement—just to name a few.

The bond markets were going crazy back then and my client base was only allowed to buy traditional "vanilla" securities such as FHLB (Federal Home Loan Bank) FNMA (Fannie Mae) FHLMC (Freddie Mac) and select corporate bonds that were rated "investment grade" securities.

On the other side of the equation were the bond traders that were wrapping jumbo pools ($200 million and above) of MBS (Mortgage Backed Securities—home loans) They were selling them on the secondary market to companies like Bear Stearns, Goldman Sachs, Lehman Brothers, Merrill

Lynch and many others. Wall Street could not buy enough of them or buy them fast enough.

However, as many of you are now aware, there was a problem. Mortgage companies started getting very creative in their loan process because the money that they were making was staggering. And I do mean staggering. With that being said, lenders came up with what is called NINAs and Stated/Stated. "NINA" stands for No Income/No Assets (meaning you did not need to verify your income or your assets) and "Stated/Stated" meant that you could simply "state" your income and "state' your assets to your lender and PRESTO--you could get approved.

What is more terrifying was that lenders were qualifying their applicants with FICO scores as low as 450. To give you a gauge, a 450 score is pitiful as credit goes. It means you have collections, late payments, possible bankruptcies and even repossessions. With all of that on one's credit report, lenders were still getting millions of people qualified, for very large amounts of money, so they could buy their dream homes. If you never knew how the mortgage industry collapsed, this was just the tip of the iceberg.

With all the news that was broadcast on these types of loans, you now know them today as being called "liar loans." People were truly "lying" about what their income and assets were so they could qualify to get a loan.

Simply put—if you could fog a mirror or sit up and take nourishment by yourself, you could qualify for a home loan. Here is where it got sticky and stupid. Many of these loans were based on floating rate securities called Adjustable Rate Mortgages, or ARMs, for short. Even today, many years after the mortgage crisis of the mid 2000's, people still cringe when hearing the words Adjustable Rate Mortgages.

An ARM differs from a fixed rate mortgage in that the interest rate moves up and down as market interest rates fluctuate. Most ARMs had that initial "fixed" rate for "x" amount of time, and they usually started with very low interest rates. It made it very attractive to Johnny and Jeannie homeowner because their mortgage payment was so ridiculously low.

I am not getting into the technicalities of how ARMs work. You get the general gist of what I am saying, and many of you reading this experienced what I am describing here. Many people lost their homes because of it. However, I will tell you this—Johnny and Jeannie homeowner bought their dream home and loved life for quite some time. Homes in California, Nevada, Florida, Arizona and other states, grew in valuation so high and appreciated so fast, millions of people then started using their homes as ATM machines. Hold on because this gets better, or worse, depending on what side of the fence you were on.

Americans started refinancing their homes and taking out the cash equity of their real estate--to the tune of billions and billions of dollars. They used the money to put in swimming pools, pay off their credit card debt (which they soon racked up again) or they made poor decisions to buy expensive new cars—all thinking in the back of their minds that the money gravy train would never end.

Here was the bad decision that Americans made, and I am citing specific examples here. If you knew that you worked in the paint department of Home Depot only making 12 bucks an hour and your spouse is making about the same hourly wage, why would you live in home that cost you a million dollars? The answer is…because you could.

The bankers, with all their power and greed, set it up that way to make them and their shareholders more money. They knew deep down in their thought process, Americans would not be able to resist the dream of homeownership—not at any cost.

Here was another problem. When you live in an expensive house and that piece of real estate starts appreciating like crazy and household income stays the same, you have the perfect recipe for disaster. The math simply does not work. Ever!

Household income MUST rise with home appreciation and valuation. If they do not, you have the potential for foreclosures. If a person's income does not rise and they refinance their home and pull out that equity in the form of cash, you now have a customer that could potentially default on his debt. Plain and simple! They cannot and will not be able to meet their debt obligations. And that is "exactly" what happened.

Let me tell you a story that happened during my career as an investment banker. I won't mention their name, not for fear of being sued, but by the time I finish this story you can pretty much narrow down who the culprit was. I had a board meeting with a huge lending company in San Francisco around 2004, and told them they were going to lose billions of dollars in their mortgage division. Guess what they did? They laughed at me.

They all thought I had lost my marbles. "Ari," as one gentleman said to me, "we are having one of the most explosive gains in real estate and the lending markets, more so than any time in the recent history of these United States. How dare you come into our offices and tell us to stop selling those loans to Wall Street!"

Now, it wasn't said to me exactly in those terms, but it was pretty much implied that I was an idiot, and that I should go back to my office and not to bother them ever again with that kind of silly gibberish.

Frankly, I was very angry after that meeting. Not because my ego was bruised, but more importantly, I knew deep down that their stupid decisions to keep funding these types of loans (and then selling them to the secondary market) was not only wrong and unethical, but the "result" of their actions would be economically crippling to the United States economy.

Why do I say this? Because math doesn't lie and the math on this was pretty darn easy to understand, wouldn't you agree? After presenting my case to these brainiacs on how income was not rising with home appreciation, they still did not get it!

When I pointed out to them that the guy working in the Home Depot paint department making 12 bucks an hour was going to lose his million dollar house when his mortgage payment adjusted, they still didn't get it. They didn't care is more like it. Go figure! Their greed had blinded them. There was no doubt about it in my mind.

Here is the interesting thing about the point I wish to make—the "dudes in the suits" thought they were making great decisions, didn't they? They strutted around their offices just as proud as peacocks saying, "Look how great we are. Look how smart we are. Look at how much money we are making for our shareholders." And, of course, "Wow! Look how much our bonus checks were last quarter. Pour the champagne! Not that crappy stuff. Get out the Crystal for cryin' out loud! After all, life is too short to drink crappy wine, right? Let the American people pay for our sloth and greed! They're idiots!"

Shareholders had huge amounts of money invested with the primary banks, and they were literally making billions of dollars. "Keep pumping those out those loans Mr. Sachs. C'mon Lehman Brothers, make us more money!" Everybody on Wall Street was on "Easy Street." And you know what? America didn't care because they were in high cotton making more money than they ever had. In fact, you could almost take a dart and throw it at the Wall Street Journal's stock page and pick a winner. Everything was moving forward, making money and going up, up and away!

Then, all of a sudden--CRASH! Now the yogurt hit the fan and the rest, as they say, is history. I certainly do not wish to live out the past and most of it is extremely painful for many people. "Ari, stop it. No more. We can't take it anymore." Okay, okay…I feel your pain. But, before I quit on this tangent, let me ask you a question. Were you one of the ones that gained, profited or had significant increases in your personal portfolio in the market during those glory years?

If the answer is yes, then guess what? I don't blame you and here's why. Our "leaders" were supposed to protect us from malfeasance and make great decisions for us all. We expected them to do their jobs and do it honestly. Yeah, I know--I'm in la-la land! Most Americans have no idea how the market works, and those that say they do either claim to be an expert or they are now behind bars.

You followed the people that made you feel safe at night when you went to bed. Hopefully the decisions they made on your behalf didn't break you or lose your entire nest egg overnight.

I don't blame you because you were not the one making those critical decisions about how best to use public money to make the most for our shareholders, our investors and our bond portfolios. I don't blame you because you just didn't know any better.

But I will blame you if you did not learn from this lesson and you travel down the same dirty road again—without thinking it through first.

Here is your next nugget for making great decisions. You must first "think" things through and understand the variables that will lead you to the outcome of that decision, and you must think of that variable "before" you act upon it.

Since we are talking about the stock market, let's use this time to serve as another example. If you are an investor, with money in hand, or it is simply burning a hole in your pocket, what questions would you ask today that you may not have asked eight or ten years ago?

You have new tools to work with, and you are also loaded down with better information today than you were yesterday, aren't you? So, what is different? The difference is that you can now make a "great decision" today better than you did yesterday. Call it wisdom or call it more gray hairs. Call it what you will, but the reality of the situation is that you cannot make a great decision if you do not know what it is you are getting into first. This is called information. Your brain requires information to assess, evaluate and understand. Your brain does this almost instantly.

For example; you see a traffic light ahead that has just turned yellow--do you slow down and then come to a stop or does your mind tell you, "You're close enough to go through before it turns red. Go ahead." That thought process requires only an instant to act upon.

You either make the decision to either go through the light or slow down to a stop. It is either one or the other. You do not stop in the middle of the intersection because you were indecisive, do you? That would be ridiculous wouldn't it? Of course it would. My point is this; you have the tools to make that split second decision because you have done it so many times before. You have the proper information.

Business Buffoonery

Before we move on to your personal life and the great decisions you need to make and how you go about doing it, let us look at more business buffoonery, as I call it. The reason for this is actually quite simple. I want you to understand how businesses are capable of doing stupid things. The result in both business and personal is exactly the same. There are two things that you must be aware of and do to make great decisions. I'll get to those two things in a moment, but humor me for a while longer and let us continue this train of thought together.

I call the following examples business buffoonery and the biggest blunders of modern time—mostly because they were not well thought out. Not even by a long shot. While I was researching this, I looked into many articles written by experts that follow business trends, cycles, and company profiles and overviews. The result of that investigation turned up basically the same blundering companies over and over again.

For the sake of argument, we have already covered the mortgage and housing crisis so we will chalk that one up to the biggest blunder of modern times since the Great Depression.

Listed below are a few of the poorest and costliest decisions from corporate America. In the long history of poor leadership and management decisions alike, a few of these also proved to be absolutely disastrous from a financial point of view. Pay attention here as there is a method to my madness, which you will soon discover! Yeah, yeah yeahhhh!

Buffoonery Blunder #1—On a New Year's Eve, in 1962, The Beatles drove through a blinding snowstorm from Liverpool, where they were playing regularly, to London. They set up their gear and knocked out about 15 tracks of songs that they were singing around the clubs in their own backyard.

They then auditioned for Dick Rowe, who was the A&R man of Decca Records. He was unimpressed with the band and told their manager, Brian Epstein, "We don't like your lads. Groups are out, especially four-piece groups with guitars, are all on their way out." He further elaborated that they sounded too much like a current band called, "The Shadows." Of course, five months later they signed with George Martin of Parlophone Records, an imprint division of EMI. This led to probably the most successful artist/producer collaboration of all time.

It reminds me of the scene in "Pretty Woman," when Julia Roberts walks into the Rodeo Drive store where she was shunned the day before and no one would wait on her. "You work on commission only, right?" she says to the snooty sales girls working the posh shop. "Why yes," states the saleswoman. Julia, holding up her shopping bags full of expensive clothes, turns to the girl and blurts out, "Big mistake. Big! Huge!"

Buffoonery Blunder #2—Way back in 1876 there was a man named William Orton who was president of Western Union. They had the monopoly on the most advanced state-of-the-art technology of the time called the telegraph. Orton was offered the patent for a new invention for the sum of the $100,000. A ton of money back then by today's standards.

The invention, of course, was the telephone. He considered the whole idea ludicrous and just plain silly. He actually wrote to Alexander Graham Bell stating, "After careful thought on your new invention, while a clever little novelty, we conclude here at Western Union, that is has no commercial possibilities whatsoever. Why would this company want to buy an electrical toy?" A few years later, the telephone took off in sales all over the world. Wow! That is a biggie.

Buffoonery Blunder #3—The Eastman Kodak Company (EK) developed the first digital camera back in 1975. Guess what they did with that technology folks? They sat on it! (They even sat on part of the technology for the cell phone as well. Ouch!) EK decided not to pursue the digital camera market as they were deathly afraid of destroying their film business, which at one point they had a 90 percent market share. After all, who would buy their film if they launched digital technology, right?

With that being said, EK didn't shoot themselves in the foot once. They did it twice! Not too long after their digital faux pas, Fuji entered the US market with lower priced film. Of course, the execs at EK chose to ignore Fuji. Why would EK's customers give up their own American home-grown company to one coming from Japan?

Can you say thrice? Yes folks, EK did it again. With the 1984 Summer Olympics being held in Los Angeles, EK turned down the premier sponsorship to be "The Official" Film of the 1984 Summer Games." Of course, Fuji slipped in at the last minute and got huge market share in an area that Kodak basically owned since the dawn of time.

"For it's one, two, three strikes you're out, at the old ball game!" Yeah, you got it. Eastman Kodak never really recovered from these, and other, stupid decisions. In 2012, the company filed for Chapter 11 bankruptcy.

Buffoonery Blunder #4—In 1991, good ole Amblin Entertainment put in a call to MARS, the chocolate company. Amblin offered MARS a cross marketing campaign so that M&M's could be used in one of their feature films and then promote the film in their own packaging designs. MARS said "No." That film was of course, "E.T., the Extraterrestrial." The rest, once again, is history. Amblin then went to Reese's Pieces, which was M&M's competitor. They said, "Yes" to Steven Spielberg and sales of Reese's Pieces jumped 65 percent within months of the film's release.

I had to save the best one for last.

Buffoonery Blunder #5 (and possibly my favorite of all time)—It was April of 1985, a day that will live in annals of marketing stupidity; and one of the biggest blunders in the history of the corporate world.

On that day, the Coca Cola Company arguably took the biggest risk in consumer goods history. It announced it had "reformulated" the most popular soft drink on the planet and introduced "New Coke" to the consumer world stage. The formula change for Coke was its first in almost 100 years.

Now I don't know about you, but I love Coke and have never been a loyal Pepsi drinker. Not that Pepsi is a bad soft drink. It's just that personally, I prefer Coke, so don't be messin' with my Coke! That was the sentiment of Coca Cola consumers all over the world. Thank goodness I was not alone in crying for my old Coke to return. People thought to themselves, *What if they bring it back? What will they call it, Old Coke?* Yuk! Who wants an old Coke, right?

No company, then or since, has seen such consumer protest for a change in one of its products. Not in any category. People were marching into stores all over the country stocking up on Coca Cola before New Coke hit the store shelves. It was sheer panic. Looting in the streets! Well, it wasn't quite that bad, but you get my point. This is the perfect example of the old saying, "If it ain't broke, don't fix it!" Can you imagine how the Chairman and CEO of the Coca Cola Company, Roberto Goizueta, felt after the world went mad? Stunned would be the one of the first words out of my mouth. The next thing I hope what went through his mind was *Oh, my God. What have we done?*

Consumer protest was so strong with all the bells and alarms going off, all over the world, it only took the Coca Cola Company 72 days to figure out they would have a riot on their hands if they did not bring back the people's favorite cola. That's sort of funny actually. "The People's Coke," as if it were a People's Choice Award. On day 73, Coca Cola brought back "Classic Coke" and the world could sleep again. It cost the bottling company tens of millions of dollars not withstanding a wild ride in its stock.

Pride and Ego

So there you have it--some of the biggest mistakes in corporate America; bad decisions chasing bad thinking. As promised, it is now time to tell you the two things that you MUST be aware of so that you may make "great decisions." They are pride and ego!

Pride and ego are your enemies when trying to make a great decision. In the examples above, those things are brick walls powerful enough to blind you from making great thoughts. In the process, it will make you stumble from making great decisions. Pride and ego are what destroyed the financial markets during the Great Depression and most recently, the housing and mortgage crisis. It was all pride and ego.

Ego is our feeling of self-worth, self-esteem, and self-importance. The ego is the organized part of our personality that gives us the perceptual defensive mechanisms and where some executive decisions are made—all from our ego.

Ego played a major role in the decision not to sign The Beatles. Dick Rowe's ego was too big, and he thought that Decca Records knew everything about recording artists because they were the best at what they did. At the time, nobody could deny that. Eastman Kodak had the same rationale. They thought they were invincible in the film industry.

What ego does is that it denies your ability to look at things from a different perspective. It blinds your judgment, your ability to reason, and your ability to use common sense.

Pride, on the other hand, is the feeling of great pleasure stemming from one's own accomplishments. Pride can also be considered in a negative connotation as it can refer to those same feelings of accomplishment derived from one's inflated sense of status, initiated from one's own accomplishments. Pride is a double-edge sword.

Some philosophers, such as Aristotle, considered pride a virtue whereas some world religious orders consider pride a sin. Proverbs 11:2 of the Old Testament speaks of pride as being one of the Seven Deadly Sins. Whatever your belief or rationalization is of pride, it is still a negative force in great decision making.

When you set off on the task of making great decisions for yourself, on a personal level, and I cannot stress this enough, you must remove your pride and your ego before doing anything. Think first about the possible results that will lead you to that decision *before* you take any action. Taking no action is also disastrous. Inaction is one's inability to make a decision, good or bad and again, the results will be negligible. Remove fear and move forward.

Let me give you an example. An athlete makes a decision to compete in an event. A true champion already sees a gold medal in his mind where someone else may just go through the paces and not see anything. He's just there to compete. The athlete that sees the gold medal has already determined his outcome. Are his chances of victory greater than those who just showed up to compete? Of course they are because his mind-set has him crossing the finish line in first place.

You have to put yourself in first place—not just now and then, but all of the time. The only way to do that is to think about your results and the possible outcome, first. And you must condition your mind and body to do it over and over again.

If you condition your mind and body to repeat the task of thinking before you make a decision and acting upon that decision, your outcome is surely to be far greater than if you leaped and then looked, right?

Let's look at it another way. What are your alternatives to your decision-making process? Are they better or worse? If you see an alternative that is better, don't you think the path of least resistance to that decision comes from the fact that you thought about your options first? Let me ask you this. What is more important to you--a decision based on the value you place upon it or the degree of difficulty it may be to obtain? An interesting conundrum, isn't it?

We place value over importance, sometimes as high as we place its degree of difficulty in obtaining it. If you tell yourself that there is no way you are ever going to get that job, is your order of importance greater or is it less? The decision not to pursue that job outweighs the value you place on going after it. You already justified in your mind that it was not worth pursuing because the feeling of your own self-importance is not that high. That would be a poor decision.

On the other hand, if you told yourself that there is no way I'm "not" getting that job, what do you think your chances are of actually pursuing it? Pretty darn good, wouldn't you think? That is a great decision. The alternative or option that you have before you now presents itself in a different light. Why is that? It is because you now have an objective in mind. A target, if you will. When you can see a target, you now have something to aim for, to shoot at. There is nothing worse than having nothing to shoot for.

So what is it you want and how do you go about getting it? It is based on a decision to take action and move forward. When you realize that you should try to determine the outcome in advance of making that decision, it may become easier for you to attain what it is you are shooting for. Of course, having a plan of action is probably a good starting point.

It is interesting when I look into recent history about some of the decisions people have made in their lives, and unbeknownst to them at the time, they changed history. On December 1, 1955 in Montgomery, Alabama, a lady named Rosa Parks refused to "give in" and would not give her seat up to move to the back of the bus. She eventually became a civil rights activist and was but one person who changed the course of those civil rights throughout the United States.

You might look back on how Martin Luther King, Jr. changed the course of history with his "I have a dream" speech. It wasn't just the speech that inspired a country—it was the great decisions that this great leader made in his life. His life marked a significant part in shaping our country's history. His tragic death defined us as a people.

I could go on and on about Rosa Parks and Martin Luther King, Jr., but my point is this—the decisions you make today could very well have a profound impact on others. That is why you must make great decisions and not just good ones. Whether you realize it or not, the decisions you make today will invariably impact someone else. Will it be for the better or for the worse? The choice is yours.

Think of the decisions you make as a map. You have many roads to follow, and if that map is clear and concise, then you should know what road you must take to get to your destination. If you take one path, you may drive off the cliff to an untimely demise. Take the other road and you will surely reach your destination safely. But what kind of map is it? Is it a financial goal map, a job goal map, a relationship map or perhaps a weight loss map? Where did you get this map? Did you make it yourself or was it supplied to you? Did you use the map of others and use that as a gauge to where you want to go?

All of these are accurate as the thinking behind it simply is that the paths on your map, as many as they may be, are designed and created by you and your decisions. A bad map or one that is not accurate or clear to read, will do what to your future? It may not be a pleasant outcome. But a good map--one that is clear, legible and can be read easily and that has focus—will lead you down a golden trail.

Oddly enough, sometimes you ignore the clearest of maps and the ones that scream to you, "Go down this path if you wish to get to your destination." You can get all the hints and all the signals so screwed up, you don't know what path to take. That is called indecisiveness.

You may very well have had someone in your life steer you off your path and your goals. It is happened to all of us at some point. You allowed your life to be dictated by someone else's decision. It may take you literally years to get back on the right path, but what decision did you make to do that?

Marriage is a great example of great decisions because you should, for the most part, be making those decisions in your life together and as a team united by a common set of beliefs and a common set of values. When those common values and beliefs are on different paths—or worse, collide—then you have more decisions to make, don't you? Do you stop the merry-go-round and get off or make the decision to stay together and work through it? This is why divorce can be so painful. In many cases, it takes years to recover, and one must make some very tough decisions henceforth in their life. I find it fascinating when you see someone with their backs totally against the wall, either financially or in a bad marriage, that they focus very hard on how to turn a bad situation into a good one. Others wallow in their own sewer and say "Oh, woe is me."

So what is the difference between those two people? There are just some people that just won't give in—like Rosa Parks. And then there are others that will continue to make bad decision after bad decision no matter what. Have you ever heard someone say to someone else, "When are you ever going to learn?" Not that that person is speaking from authority—they usually say something like that to make themselves feel good, because they're not never going learn, either! Takes one to know one, right?

I find it interesting when people try to make others feel bad when their own life doesn't turn out like they think it should. That should be your defining moment. That point in your life when you have an "AH-HA" moment and say to yourself, "OK, now I get it! I better start making some better decisions in my life from now on so I don't repeat that stupid mistake."

Now you're on to something my friends. Well, guess what? Everybody has a defining moment in their lives. You have a moment, however brief or long it is, to make a change for the better. The question that you need to ask yourself is—do you recognize the signals and know what to look for when that light bulb moment comes along?

After speaking to thousands of people from all over the world, I know deep down that God (or whatever higher power you call upon) gave us the wherewithal to determine right from wrong. We have the ability to make some awesome decisions in our lives, and we also have the ability to destroy ourselves by making very poor ones. But the great thing about that is you now know you have the ability to try to predict your future by thinking things through first. By looking at the variables of potential outcomes, and based on those potential outcomes, you are on your way to making great decisions!

There is one last thought I wish to make before we move on to the next chapter. When you make a decision of high importance (choosing the right golf club doesn't count), you must be "determined" to take some type of action towards that all important decision.

Determination will always lead you to a solution. Determination will always cause you to take some type of action, and determination will always cause some type decision to be made. Improper action or a bad decision will usually lead to poor results or possible failure. But even with failure, a new decision should lead you one step closer to success. You now have the perspective to make a more intelligent decision towards a better goal or intention.

If you are determined, have the right mental focus and are determined that you will take positive action, you should be able to make great decisions. You can either make a decision to destroy your world, or build it and make it stronger!

"To make a great decision you must remove two disastrous elements: pride and ego. When these are entered into the equation, wars have started, empires have fallen, and civilizations have crumbled. Never allow pride and ego to enter in making great decisions. The results are sure to be poor!"

Aristides Priakos

Principle #2

Be Better Tomorrow Than You Were Today

One of the great "thinkers" of current day that I have had the pleasure to study was a gentleman by the name of Jim Rohn. Jim was one of the pioneers of personal development, a wonderful teacher and a great author. He started his seminar tours back in 1963 when people barely knew or even understood what personal development was all about.

I think the only thing people could compare it to was what they knew of Dale Carnegie's "How to Win Friends and Influence People," or Napoleon Hill's "Think and Grow Rich." By the way, if you have never read those two books, and you have a thirst to be a better human being, they should be mandatory reading for you.

Jim Rohn authored dozens of personal development books, tapes and DVDs throughout the course of his life. He was a fascinating man, full of wisdom and a great orator. His passing in 2009 marked the end of an era of great self-help coaches of the time, and he was one of the main reasons I started on a path of personal development. We will miss him terribly, but he lives on through all his works.

There is a wonderful story Jim told his many audiences. Many years ago, when he was newly married, his front doorbell rang at his home. He opened the door and there before him stood a Girl Scout. She was, of course, selling the yearly traditional cookies of the same name. She was the cutest thing. She proceeded to sell him on the merits of buying her cookies, the various flavors of all the tasty morsels in her basket, and the benefits she would receive for selling the most cookies during that season.

He was sold right from the get go. She was just adorable and her enthusiasm and passion for selling her cookies was just fantastic. *She was a natural born salesperson,* Jim thought to himself. He told this cute little girl that he had already stocked up on Girl Scout cookies the day before, but he hoped to be able buy from her next year. The little girl was most polite and she thanked Jim for his time, and told him to have a great day. Unfortunately, the problem was at that particular point in his life, Jim was flat broke and could not afford the two dollars that she requested for her wares. He felt terrible that he had lied to her.

As Jim recalls the story many years later, "What was it that happened in my life that I could not afford just two measly dollars to buy Girl Scout cookies? What makes matters worse is that I had to lie to a Girl Scout!" Of course, the audience laughs, but to Jim it wasn't funny at the time. He elaborates, "That is the day I told myself I do not want to live like this anymore!"

If you are a person that is in a similar kind of position and you are so sick and tired of being sick and tired, something inside you "snaps!" You can reflect back on that day and declare it as one of the most defining moments in your life. Many of us have hit rock bottom. There are some that truly don't know what rock bottom is, and there are others that may never hit rock bottom.

My point is this—somewhere, sometime or somehow you will realize that you need to do something in your life to make a change for the better, even if you do not hit rock bottom. One should not have to wait around to change one's life because one has not hit rock bottom. When you figure out what it is you need to change, you must then proceed to do it every day for the rest of your life. It is not as easy as it sounds, but also not impossible to achieve. You will have to constantly train and condition your brain to keep sending it messages from the memories that you store in your head.

Those memories will give you a reference point for what you need to do to be better tomorrow. Later in this chapter, I am going to describe to you how powerful memories are, and what they can do to help you become better; but first, I want to tell you what happened to me many years ago.

My Painful Memory

I hope what I am about to share with you registers and may also trigger and touch something very emotional for you because there was a time in my life I hit rock bottom--big time. It was an extremely painful time in my life, and a type of pain that I never wish to relive or experience ever again.

I was living in California, and I was having a miserably tough time looking for work. I was an investment banker, but I had taken some time off to start a business. I just could not make it go like I had wanted. I started losing money left and right as my income relied solely on this business. I was living in a nice apartment and, of course, being in California it was not cheap. But I stayed there anyway thinking that it was just a matter of time before my business would ignite, and I'd be fine again financially.

As the days and then months progressed, I found myself getting deeper into debt, and digging myself into a financial hole so deep I could not see myself getting out of it. That reminds me of one of America's famous cowboy and Western stars who was a gentleman by the name of Will Rogers. He was known for one of his memorable quotes, "When you find yourself in a hole, quit digging."

Well, I was digging myself a pretty big-size hole, and I was digging deeper and deeper and deeper. No one was there to throw me rope, either. It didn't even look like a hole anymore. It looked more like a scene out of "The Abyss."

I'm a Christian, of Greek Orthodox descent, and have always believed in my faith in God and my savior Jesus Christ. So I prayed and prayed and prayed for a miracle to happen to help my business, and to help me get over these financial woes. Things didn't change. They got worse. I was a few months away from getting thrown out of my apartment, very close to getting my car repossessed, and I had no money to buy food.

I had to get a job quickly, but the thought of doing that made me sick to my stomach. I don't know about some of you, but it has always left a bitter taste in my mouth to work for other people. You just don't have any control over your own destiny, and why would you want to make other people rich when you can do it yourself? Something wasn't working in my life and I knew it. But I figured that I would get a job for a while so I could at least put some food on the table, and maybe hold off the landlord a while longer.

The economy was just puttering along and putting out the feelers with prospective employers was not only time consuming, but expensive. Printing up resumes, going on job interviews and all the car expenses, time and what-not, was not cheap.

At this point I had not paid my gas bill in many months, so the bastards shut it off. Go figure—they wanted money for their service? I never heard of such a thing. Yeah, I can laugh about it now.

I had to heat up water in a big casserole dish on the stove, carry it full of hot water directly to my shower. I was very creative in how I bathed with alternating the casserole dish, a washcloth, cold water and mixing the two together so I could at least take a tepid sponge bath. Pretty bleak you would say? Well, it got worse.

About the time that I am praying and not wanting to rely on any more favors from my friends, I got into a state where I was very depressed. I wasn't happy with myself, I could not believe that I was in a situation like this, and I was just about as miserable as a human being could be.

I wasn't taking care of myself, and I looked like a truck had run over me, and then backed up and rolled over me again. On top of that, I only had two dollars left to my name. Not two dollar bills, mind you--two dollars in change with a whole lot of nickels, dimes and pennies.

When Jim Rohn talked about not having the two dollars to buy Girl Scout cookies, I could most certainly relate to that story. I was starving and had two dollars to my name. What the hell was I going to do?

It was raining cats and dogs in California—one of those months where it just would not let up. Every day it seemed to rain harder and harder. Californians call it "The Pineapple Express" because the weather systems come straight into Northern California directly from Hawaii—thus the term Pineapple! These particular weather patterns shoot right over the Pacific Ocean from the Hawaiian Islands, slam right into the coast of California, and then it find their way right up the Sierra Nevada's. It's where we get most of our snow pack for the year. And when it rains, it rains hard!

That night, around 2 a.m., as the rain was coming down in buckets, someone started pounding on my front door. "Who the hell could that be?" I asked myself. But I already knew what it probably was all about. I slowly opened the front door, and standing there was a man in a raincoat, shielding his head from the pounding rain. "I'm here to take possession of your vehicle," he said. I lowered my head in shame. "I know," I said. He then told me, "I'll need your keys now please. If there is anything you need to get out of the trunk of your car, this would be a good time to do so." I nodded. But who the heck would want to go out in the pouring rain to retrieve what little belongings I had in my car.

I told him to hold on a moment. I went back into one of my bedrooms, collected the car keys and handed it over to him without incident. There was nothing else I could do at that point. He thanked me for not trying to put up any argument with him, and I said something stupid back to him like, "Yeah—whatever." I wasn't even mad. Take the damn car was my attitude at this point. I shut the door and immediately went to my bedroom. I was so exhausted I could not even think anymore, and went to sleep almost instantly.

The next day was going to be the worst day of my entire life, and one that I will also never forget for the rest of my life. I find it interesting that some memories are so stinking strong that they will leave a lasting impression in your mind until the day you die. When those memories are recalled from the memory banks in your brain, some of them seem like they happened just yesterday.

That is exactly what happened on the worst day of my life. The events that happened on that day carved a memory in my subconscious so powerful I will remember it until the day I leave this earth.

When I woke up that next morning, I was thinking how hungry I was and what I was going to eat with my two dollars. I then remembered my car was repossessed the previous evening. There is something else I failed to mention to you. When I told you I went to bed last night, I actually slept on my bedroom floor. I no longer had any bedroom furniture whatsoever. No mattress, nightstand or bureaus—all gone. I also did not have any living room furniture, dining room table, coffee table, chairs, televisions or any other of the creature comforts—all were gone. I had to sell all of that stuff just to keep going and survive. I basically had nothing else to sell. The only thing that remained in my place was my office desk, my computer, and my phone. That was it!

I lived down the street from a fairly busy intersection, but without a car it was about a 15-minute walk. You may say to yourself, "that's nothing." And you are right. A 15-minute walk or jog is excellent exercise, but I wasn't going out to get exercise. I was only in survival mode at this point. I was going on a 15-minute walk down to the Shell station to get a 99 cent hotdog, a drink and maybe a chocolate bar or something sweet. Thanks to my mother, I have a huge sweet-tooth…always have.

I needed to recount my change, go through my desk again just to see if I left any pennies around. Pennies when you are flat, stupid broke still add up to millions of dollars if you have enough of them. That is truly what I was thinking to myself. I actually found a few more pennies and a few more nickels and dimes. My total net worth was about two dollars and fifty seven cents.

With the rain still coming down, I needed to get myself motivated to walk the 15 minutes to the Shell station to get food. I still had my clothes, thank God, and also had some decent raingear to protect myself from all the "pineapples" that God was still throwing at California.

I got dressed and headed out into the elements. Have you ever seen the wind blow so hard during a rainstorm that the water moves sideways? That was what it was like. The rain was falling to earth sideways. *How bizarre is that?* I thought to myself. Without my raingear on I would have already been soaked to the core.

I left the complex gate and started walking down the street, but here is the interesting thing I remember about leaving my apartment that day. In my place, at least I was safe. Even without any furniture or food, I was still safe being inside because no one could get to me and I was protected from the elements of nature.

Out in the open and leaving my little Camelot, if you will, I was lost in the forest. When I walked out of those gates, it was survival of the fittest. The rain was flooding the streets and there were parts of the road that we completely under water. It was so deep in some parts of the street that when the cars drove slowly past me, it created a small tsunami of water rolling that flowed right over the curb with ease. Even though my body remained relatively dry, my feet were soaked right through my tennis shoes. My sadness and despair was so strong and so deep I began to cry. What did I do to get myself into this position? What terrible decisions did I make to get me to the point where I had no car, no furniture, and no money? What terrible decisions did I make in my life that I was walking in the middle of a torrential downpour to a gas station down the road to get a hotdog? I stopped dead in my tracks and just let the rain hit the top of my head and my face.

What made matters worse is that I now remembered what today was. It was Christmas morning! I had my car repossessed on Christmas Eve and today, Christmas, I am walking to a Shell station to spend my last two dollars and fifty seven cents on food.

I started balling like a boy that has just been beaten up by the school bully. The rain was coming down so hard you could not differentiate my tears from rain drops. To me, they were both the same. I looked up into the heavens and started praying. "God, help me. I am broken, and I need your help. Please watch over me right now as I am in my darkest hour. Send your angels down to protect me from the evil that surrounds me. I ask that you help me make the right decisions henceforth; and I know that you will help me out of this darkness so things will be better tomorrow than they are today."

I just could not stop crying. However, at some point walking in the rain, a sense of relief came over me as I knew things would get better. How could they get any worse, right? I have had conversations with other people about this time in my life, and many have told me that they had it worse than I. Some were homeless, had lost their limbs or were surviving under a bridge. They had to survive without any aid from anyone else. I do understand and know full well that some people have indeed been through worse, but that is not the point here. The point is that I am sharing with you the day that was my darkest hour—the day I hit rock bottom and the events that occurred to get me where I am today.

Somehow I managed to forge on and get to the store. When I in walked in to the store, I noticed all the Christmas decorations, but my attention was immediately drawn to the music playing in the background. It was "O Holy Night." I don't know about you, but when I hear that wonderful Christmas song, it completely moves me. It doesn't matter what religious belief you have, it is just a magnificent piece of music.

I thought the angels were singing when I heard that blasting over the radio. My attitude shifted almost immediately as I felt a huge burden was being lifted from my shoulders. As if my prayers had been answered and God heard me cry out to him with the greatest of sincerity and earnest.

To this day, a tad over 20 years later, I still remember the pain I was in; and, of course, when I hear "O Holy Night" I cannot help but think about the day that I spoke to a higher power, and that my prayers were answered. And yes, I usually shed a tear or two with that memory so deeply embedded in my subconscious.

I stood in that store and was able to procure two bean and cheese burritos that were on sale, two for one. I got a soda and a candy bar, and still walked out of there with a few pennies in my pocket. Back into the rain I trekked back, plastic bag in one hand and my soda in the other. I was starving, but the walk back home was completely different than it was on the way to the store. At least I had a warm home to go back to, and I could put something in my belly.

Here is the interesting thing about that day. I succumbed to the moment and was in a place where I called upon a higher power, my Lord Jesus Christ, and asked him to help me. Again, I am not pushing religion on anyone here, but I know many of you that have been in a situation where perhaps you have been in a very dark place, feared for your life, or had someone going through a life-threatening surgery—you prayed.

Without belaboring the story, and me getting to the point of the story quicker, I remember that particular Christmas was on a weekend. Here is the coolest part of what happened to me. If you recall earlier in the chapter, I was looking for work and was sending out resumes like a madman.

On the Monday after Christmas, early in the morning, I received a phone call from a vice president of a very large financial institution. He apologized for bothering me over the holiday weekend (if he only had any idea) and asked if I had a few minutes to chat. "Of course," I said to him. Again, he apologized for bothering me over Christmas, but he told me that his firm had received my resume.

I immediately froze there solid. *Why would this guy call me on a major holiday to tell me anything but good news*, I thought to myself. *Please, please, please--offer me a job.* I repeated that over and over again in my head in that nanosecond before he said to me, "We think you are perfect for the position, and I wanted to personally call you and offer you the job over the holiday as we need you to start first thing on Monday after New Year's Day. I could not believe my ears. "Are you serious?" I said to him. I was speechless for a moment and the silence between that question and his next comment seemed like forever. "Well, I was hoping to make your day by offering you the job, and we simply could not wait until next Monday to tell you as we needed to give you enough notice. Are you available to start at that time? We're very sorry to give you such short notice."

Are you kidding me? I thought to myself. *Don't be coy Ari— just say yes to the man and let's get on with your life.* As you probably can guess I said yes to the man, hung up the phone and started weeping. "Thank you God for answering my prayers. I promise to never allow myself to ever be in a position like I was in during this holiday season." I could not stop saying thank you enough. I was truly blessed.

Talk about seeing someone who was walking on cloud nine. You should have seen me. Just a few short hours earlier I was in despair, walking in the rain, dead broke and thought the world was going to end. Now, the sun is shining, and life is fantastic! God is great, and I am ready to conquer anything that comes my way. Amazing what attitude does, and how fast it can shift from negative to positive. I will never forget that as I look on those days as a very valuable lesson.

Our Own Painful Past

If it moves others into action and I can connect with anyone reading this book, then understand this—nothing... I mean nothing, ever stays the same. Things will always change, and it is up to you to make the best of the situation and don't ever quit. If I had not been sending out my resume like crazy, I would not have been in a position to receive that phone call that changed my life. Had I not done some type of activity to be better from one day to the next, my life might very well have taken on a different course.

So, now that you have read a little bit about my story, you might be asking yourself, "what the hell does any of this nonsense have to do with the title of this chapter?" Unfortunately, I had to go the long way to get back to dead center, but hopefully you get the gist of what I am about ready to tell you.

The reality of situation is that in order to be better tomorrow than you were today, you must understand where you are at this particular moment in your life—and truly find out if you are happy with your life at this exact moment in time. Are you truly happy? Are you a happy person full of life and cheer and love; or are you down, negative in your thinking, and sad all the time?

Here is the enlightening part of what I am about to share with you. Don't call this a secret to happiness, but call it more of an awareness of what you need to do to become better tomorrow than you were today. You already possess the tool to be better tomorrow than you were today, and that tool is in your head. That tool is called your memory.

Everything we do in our lives, all that we know and how we act present and future, how we interact, socialize and gather together as a people, is all connected to our memories. Good, bad or indifferent, everything that we know up to this point, and how we behave, is all based on the memories of our past. The way we behave today is based on a memory of how we were raised.

Some memories are painful, and some are pleasurable. Some memories leave a lasting impression while others you have to try really hard to recall. The interesting thing about this is that every single human being on the planet has experienced all of the above.

How you handle that memory and how you react to it is everything! It affects your mind-set, and it also affects all those around you. Memories affect your heart in how we love each other, and also how we can be cruel to one another.

We associate our current mind-set and mood with painful or pleasurable memories of our past. These are the reference points we need assess and gauge how we act today and what actions and steps we will take tomorrow.

Memories are our lifeblood. They are the rule book of how we parent, how we love, how we care for each other, how we communicate with one another, and how we interact with one another. Memories are how we behave around others, how we behave towards others, and how we hurt others. No one on the face of the earth can take your memories away from you. They cannot be stolen or bought, and they cannot be traded or bartered, but they can be shared. One of the most beautiful things we do as humans is to share our memories with each other.

We even share death with each other; and death is probably one of the most powerful memories that we have, isn't it? We have all experienced death in some fashion and at some point in our lives—it is just a part of life. We might look at a dearly departed loved one and think back. *What would they do in a situation like this?*

Between dedicating the last book to my mother, and to the point in time where I finished writing this one, my loving mother Penelope passed away at the tender age of 91. She was an amazing woman who always told me that nothing ever stays the same, and that I should never quit and never give up on my dreams. My memories of her death and her words of wisdom to me are a very powerful image burned into my subconscious memory banks.

None of wish to dwell on our own mortality, but many times the memories of our departed loved ones may very well carry you through your darkest hours. Have you ever talked to a family member after they have passed? I have. Perhaps not in the physical sense, but I have found myself talking to my mother and my father. I've asked them to help guide me and to give me strength throughout certain times in my life. I think it was more like trying to gain access to their wisdom more than anything else.

Many of you might have done the same thing. It is what makes us human. We need that connection to our past. We always have and we always will. It is a reference point of what we may use to justify our actions to do something in our future. Using our past experiences and memories is the way you can now gauge how you can be better tomorrow than you are today.

Let me give you an example. Take a moment right now and think of an early memory of when you were a child. Can you remember a holiday like Christmas or Hanukkah or maybe one of your birthday parties? Can you remember an event with a brother or sister, a vacation you might have had, or maybe even your first family pet?

All the above, for the most part, are or should be, joyous experiences and memories. Unless your house burned down on Christmas Day, God forbid, your memories of your childhood should be pleasant. Or were they the opposite?

Did you have memories of being spanked, getting into trouble, being sexually or physically abused? Do you remember being beaten, or having a parent—or both parents—who were alcoholics? Did you come from a divorced home, or were you orphaned?

In either scenario—pleasurable memory or painful memory—it gives you the ability or association. You have been given the ability to tell your story through your memories, and you have been given the ability to recognize patterns and very specific situations.

But there is something greater at play here. Our memories give us the ability to do something really incredible. They give us the ability to recognize right from wrong. That is the key to your universe, and the one that will open up the lock for you to be better tomorrow than you were today.

You know from a memory or an event in your life what is and what is not acceptable in our society; and from the "rules" of your life, the difference between what is right and what is wrong. From that, you can now differentiate what you need to do to be better tomorrow than you were today. This is one of the most important principles on how I live my life. I am always trying to figure out a way to be better one day from the next.

It is very interesting how fast your memory bank works. I'll give you an example. If you hear a piece of music, how fast might your brain be flooded with memories associated with that piece of music in a period of time when you first heard it? It can bring up all kinds of emotional memories for you, from the music you heard when you first fell in love to the music you heard when a family member died. Memories are the way that our brain indexes our life, much like a library. You can instantly recall a memory by the way it is indexed in your brain.

With that being said, you should also be able to know what you need to do to be better tomorrow than you are today. After all, your ability to index and pull out the right information will help guide you to be better.

I want to play close attention to the word "information." That is exactly what your memory does for you—it gives you information. Good, bad or indifferent, your brain constantly sends you information from a memory that you have indexed in your brain. Something interesting may happen to you with the right information. It may help you continue and move forward, or it may make you quit. One may be pleasurable while the other may be very painful.

While in the process of inventing the light bulb, Thomas Edison tried several thousand times to find the right filament that would work in the housing of the bulb. When others pointed out how many times he failed, Thomas Edison replied, "I didn't fail. I just found out several thousand ways how 'not' to make a light bulb."

Thomas Edison had the right information, and the next day he made it better than it was the day before, and so on and so on. If he had quit, it may have taken many more years than it did to invent the light bulb. The right information, a never-quit attitude, and his ability to be better tomorrow than he was the previous day changed the world forever.

One of the most fascinating things about memories is that they give you the ability to expand and collapse time. Think about it for a minute. Your brain, being the supercomputer that it is, is also time machine. When you tell a story to someone, you are recalling a memory. By recalling that memory, you are instantly collapsing time by the recollection of that memory. The memory may be when you were a child, but you are telling that story to another person as if it were yesterday. It is like time travel, and it is also easy to do, isn't it?

Your memories chart every detail of your entire life. So with that being the said, your ability to be better tomorrow than you were today should be relatively easy. It should be because your memories also shape you and help identify you with others. Your memories are you!

So if you know who you are at this particular moment in time, in this exact moment in your history, then you have the ability to know what you need to do to be better tomorrow than you are today.

Every day creates new memories which bring freshness to the universe. An idea, or thought, comes from being conscious and that consciousness will determine a positive or negative contribution to the universe. Which one are you contributing?

If you strive to be better tomorrow than you were today, then you must first realize what is, or what will be, your contribution? If it your intentions to be a better criminal or thief tomorrow—that is not a positive contribution to the universe. If that is your intention then I am glad you are reading this book.

To be better tomorrow than you were today will require you to define your moment; it will actually make you stop and think what will be a good thing to do. You must have that moment clearly defined to be able to decide what it is you wish to make better. What is it that defines you as a person? What is it that you wish to put out there into the universe that will make a positive impact in your life and the lives of others? It is very, very important that you get this, so I will repeat it once again. What is it that you will make better tomorrow and place into the universe that will positively impact your life, and the lives of those around you?

"Putting it out there," so to speak, is not what I am after here ladies and gentlemen—what my goal and hope for you is that you truly understand that in order to be better tomorrow than you were today, you must have purpose.

There must be an objective in mind. Remember you are trying to be better every day for the rest of your life; therefore, every day will bring a whole new set of goals.

Your memories will help you determine what you need to do to be better tomorrow because a memory after all is just a snapshot of a certain time in your life. Those memories or snapshots, whether you like it or not, will most certainly define who you are as a person; and what you will do in your own future that will ultimately affect how you treat others.

Better Suggestions

As I close this chapter with you, I would like it if you wrote down on a piece of paper what your objective is to be better tomorrow. Writing things down on paper will give a sense of clarity and purpose. It will become real for you if you can see it on paper. It should drive you to do a few very simple things to change your life and the lives of those around you. Do you wish to become a better parent? Then write down how you propose to do that. Will you listen to your children more attentively? Will you try to not go flying off the handle if they do something that sets you off? Can you be more tolerant towards others? How about giving more to your church or temple? Are you contributing to the world positively? What can you do to be better?

I think most would agree that in order for us to be better we must first understand your self-awareness in the "now." What is your current behavior and how do you cope with things like love, loss of a loved one, or a job transition? How do you cope with your marriage during the tough times, and how do you react towards others when they make a comment or do something that irritates you? Do you get mad or get even? Or do you let it go and just consider the source of their comments or anger?

All of these things listed above are how you react to the here and now. That alone will determine the steps you need to take to become better tomorrow.

Having someone you look up to and respect is also a great reference point of becoming a better person. Do you have a work associate that you like being around? If you see someone act kind towards others, and they treat them as an equals, it sets a great example to follow in their footsteps, doesn't it? Kindness beats the heck out of being mean and abusive.

Reading about successful people and their teachings is yet another way to better yourself. As a student of personal development and now as an author, I am constantly trying to find new ways to improve my mind and my soul by feeding my brain only good food. Good stuff in, good stuff out. When I hear or read other people's stories and I listen or see how they achieved greatness after overcoming great adversity, I'm in awe of the human element that pushes us and drives us to be better. It inspires me to be better. If you think that you are the only one with problems and you are stuck in a rut, think about those less fortunate than you. There are so many stories about people who came from relative obscurity that made something of themselves when they were once nothing.

Find stories like that to read, and watch, and observe, others with whom you consider a role model. What do they do? How do they behave, and how do they treat others? The results should not be that shocking to you. It all boils down to one thing and one thing only—how better do you wish to become?

Here are my ten suggestions to help you get started on your path of betterment.

1) Be more tolerant for it is so easy to argue.
2) Practice patience and self-control as it will comfort and soothe you over time.
3) Be more empathetic as there are far too many cold-hearted people in the world.
4) Remove jealousy for it is destructive, and it compounds insecurity.
5) Get rid of anger for it is the work of evil.
6) Be kind to others for the rewards in return are rich.
7) Be easy to forgive as the ability to show mercy and compassion is the teaching from God.
8) Watch what you say and how you say it as once spoken, it can never be retracted.
9) Show people that you truly care about them and place their feelings above yours, and they will give back ten-fold.
10) Be ever so thankful for what you have as weeping over absence solves nothing.

It starts with your attitude, your focus of what you want and what you believe in. but you must first believe in yourself to accomplish your goals. And in order to accomplish that you must take the first step of being better tomorrow than you were today.

"There is nothing noble in being superior to your fellow man; true nobility is being superior to your former self."

Ernest Hemingway

Principle #3

Be of the Highest of Integrity

This is a chapter that was probably the easiest to write, but some of the concepts that I will share with you are brain twisters. Some of them just simply defy logic. First of all, let us see what the definition is from the dictionary.

Webster's definition—*Integrity: the quality of being honest and having strong moral principles, moral uprightness. It's the state of being whole and undivided.*

I would like for you to concentrate on the word "whole" from the above definition just for a minute. Whole in this sense means that you must be whole as a person and have a keen understanding of self. Every bit of you, your core being, and the sum of who you are as a person must be "whole."

To do that one must comprehend what position your heart and mind are in right now and what you use to gauge if you are of high integrity. What are you composed of? What makes you tic? What is your make-up, your texture? Some people believe they have integrity because they do good things for others. Doing good things for others does not mean you have integrity. It just means you like helping others. Not a bad thing, but it doesn't mean you have integrity.

Anyone can place lipstick on a pig. It is still a pig! Anyone can claim they have integrity, and most people think they act with integrity. Unfortunately, being of the highest integrity lacks dearly in our society. Let me give you an example. Do you think Wall Street acts with the highest of integrity? After what we have been through with the financial crisis in the mid to late 2000s, with tremendous loss in pension funds, executives making millions of dollars (billions in some cases), and the incredible amount of fraud that took place—is there any integrity left on Wall Street? Your first response would be to say, "Hell no!"

That may very well be the case, but there are plenty of people with high integrity that know the difference between right and wrong that work on Wall Street. I know many of them, and they cringe at the thought of having to be placed in a barrel full of rotten apples. Yes, some of my friends on Wall Street made millions. That doesn't mean that they weren't honest and dealt with great integrity.

Have you ever met someone that you know is unscrupulous, that has no ethics whatsoever, and made a lot of money? You might say to yourself, "I can't believe that SOB made so much money. All he did was screw people all the way up the corporate ladder, and now look at him. He thinks he's king of the mountain!"

He may very well be king of the mountain for now, but I promise you that the universe does not work that way, nor will it allow the continuation of bad to thrive. Remember this always—evil never, ever wins in the long run! It will catch up to them. Maybe not now or not even in the next few years, but not being of the highest integrity will someday be their downfall, and they will fall from grace and will then be mountain goats.

Write this down: It is NOT up to you to correct that. Dishonesty will always find a way to rear its ugly head; and it will take care of itself, in its own time, and will eventually justly take care of those that are evil.

You may think that the Bernie Madoffs of the world need a whistle blower. And you would be right. But nobody knew and no one in their right mind was going to take this man down. First of all, he got away with it for years--many, many years. Secondly, he was making people a lot of money.

It was on paper, of course, but they didn't know that at the time. This is part of the brain twister that blows me away about Bernie Madoff. This man was the former head of the NASDAQ (National Association of Securities Dealers Automated Quotations).

Here is the kick in the head. While operating his elaborate Ponzi scheme throughout the world, he is simultaneously giving lectures to some of Wall Street's biggest executives explaining to them how to look for fraud in the marketplaces. Not only did he tell them how to look for it, he even showed them what to look for. He was the biggest perpetrator of fraud and he did it right underneath their noses. Wow! What balls!

This guy is bilking billions of dollars from his investors, robbing from Peter to pay Paul, and has the audacity to lecture and speak on the exposure of fraud right to his peers. And they thought he walked on water. Idiocy! I bet there are many of you that never knew that about him. But can you imagine the chutzpah? That just blows me away. That is one of the best examples I can think of about not being of the highest integrity. Ya think?

Of course, we all know the rest of the story, some fifty billion dollars later and the destruction of so many lives in the process. To go back to the start of this chapter we can tell that Bernie was never "whole." He acted selfishly and with mal intent to defraud the public to maintain his elaborate lifestyle, and gosh only knows what else.

I have not had a chance to speak to Bernie Madoff nor do I care to, but I would like to ask him one question if I were ever to ever interview him. "What were you thinking the whole time you were stealing?" I'd like to hear that answer, but it matters not. He has a lot of time to think about it from behind bars, doesn't he?

Let us continue our study of being of the highest of integrity. I heard someone describe themselves one time as "being too honest." I kind of chuckled when I heard that and he asked me why I laughed. I said, "One can never be too honest. You either are or you are not." He nodded his head back to me and smiled in agreement.

My point is that many people truly believe that they are honest, and they really do not know any better. These are some of the same people that hold up the Bible in one hand and preach the gospel while fondling children with the other hand, and then claim they didn't do anything of the kind.

What the hell kind of behavior and thinking process is that? That is not being of the highest integrity…that is just plain disgusting and truly evil. They hide behind the good book for protection as that is how their mind justifies such terrible acts.

Let me get back on track here as my mind goes faster than my fingers can type. I thank you for following me on the wild Aristides train of thought. Some years back I wrapped my head around the concept of having a common set of values and a common set of beliefs, but there are vast differences between the two. Let me explain.

People use both values and beliefs to achieve the actions of their behavioral patterns, but they still are different. You could use religion as a belief system, and whatever your spiritual belief system is, that is yours to hold and keep. For the lesson here, I will state that beliefs are a way of conviction without having proof of that belief.

Even though we hold true the belief that all men are created equal, we do not necessarily share the same thought process. We no longer need any evidence in a belief that all men are created equal regardless of gender, race, sex, creed, religion or education. Those that disagree with that statement and declare that all men are not created equal have racist and sexist values. That is just one example of the difference between values and beliefs.

Beliefs are how we view our own world and those that occupy it. Our values grow like branches on a tree, based on those belief systems that we have developed and conceived in our mind. Some of these beliefs are based on what we perceive from our past values. Isn't that interesting? You can believe in one thing, but have different values about that belief.

You may encounter some experience in your life that will challenge the value you previously held on a particular belief. You may have had a loved one so very close to death, yet they recovered from all odds and they are alive today. You may have previously never believed in a higher power like God, but perhaps your views and the belief that God exists greatly changed when that loved one recovered from a terminal illness.

Someone told me one time that they never believed in God, but found it interesting that when his little girl was going to have major surgery, he found himself praying to God for her recovery. She did indeed pull through, and today he is a God-fearing man. Was it his value or belief in God that changed? Both changed. His newly placed belief in God changed because his value that he placed in that belief changed. He "believed" that his daughter pulled through because of prayer. The value he placed on that belief—that it was God that helped his daughter gave him great clarity and conviction to his new belief in God. Confused? Don't be. It gets easier.

"Whoa, Nellie! Ari! What the heck does this have to do with integrity?" That is a great question and you will have to humor me for a bit longer, be patient and all will become clear.

Understanding what your beliefs and values might be is a very important key component to your own personal development. The "core values" and the things you feel are very important to you, such as honesty, equality, loyalty, being faithful and your code of conduct. These affect us all at a very deep subconscious level, and we use these values to make many decisions on a daily basis.

Your beliefs, on the other hand, are based on assumptions of what we read, see, hear, and think about various things. Like how we see ourselves and how we react to others. They can also be based on factual evidence. I know that the sun will rise in the east and set in the west. That is a fact, so I believe it. Because the sun has been doing that consistently for billions of years, it gives me a sense of value as I like to sit in the sun by the beach. My values are kind of selfish when it comes to sun tanning I must say. Shame on me, huh?

One of the interesting things you will find about your values and beliefs is that over time, they will change. You are constantly shifting and rearranging your belief system, sometimes on a subconscious level. You might have had a business partner that cheated you out of money for example. Does that mean you stop conducting business? No. It simply means that your beliefs changed on how you may value future partners or if you choose to have a partner at all. That sets a new belief system for you.

What about a cheating spouse? What does that do to your belief system, and the values that held true for the person that cheated on you? They change dramatically, don't they?

Sharing With Others

When you have conviction about a belief and that belief is so strong and so powerful, what is it that you see yourself doing? You share that belief with others, don't you? For example, you may feel strongly about a particular candidate that is running for political office. You agree with the exact same beliefs and values this candidate presents to the public. You start to work for this person because you feel that they are the best person for the job. It is also based on the fact that you made the conscious decision to stand by their side and help them get elected.

During the campaign, you find out that this person has cheated on their spouse with a member of the staff. What does this now do to your conviction of values and beliefs? If you have strong moral character and are "whole" then it should turn your stomach. What would you do?

Would you continue to work for them or quit? We are human so it can be said logically that you would now be judgmental of this person. The belief you had in his values have now changed, haven't they? You have every right to be judgmental. Again, what would you do? Think about it for a minute. If you have a core belief system in place and all of a sudden that core belief system dramatically shifts for you, because of the adulterous affair this person had, would you then voice your displeasure or keep it to yourself and move on with your life? Interesting situation isn't it?

I remember a long time ago I was playing golf with a buddy of mine at his prestigious "members only" country club in California. That day, my friend introduced me to someone of great business influence. Coincidently, I had called on this man's company for business prior to meeting him that day. We exchanged handshakes and some general pleasantries, but that was about it. After playing a round we adjourned into the clubhouse for an adult beverage. My buddy and I were discussing the piss-poor round of golf we just played when I noticed the person of influence walk into the clubhouse. He had just finished his round as well.

I turned to my buddy and asked him what he thought about the person of influence. His comment to me was one I didn't see coming. "I'd never do business with him, let's put it that way," he said. I turned to my friend with a look of puzzlement. Here I was hoping to meet this person of influence, who from what I heard was a very successful man, made millions of dollars and gave much to charity.

I asked my buddy, "Why do you say that?" He leaned over to me and said, "He cheats at golf?" What he said next I will never forget, and it was a great lesson for me to learn. My friend went on to say, "He also cheats on his wife. As a matter of fact, some of the women members you see in this clubhouse right now have slept with him, and his wife doesn't even know it."

I was stunned to learn of such news. I stupidly said, "I just don't get it." My friend turned to me, "Let me ask you a question Ari." I said, "Okay, go ahead." He leaned further in to me, his voice lower, "If it is that easy for a person to cheat at golf and cheat on his wife, how easy might you think it would be for him to cheat you in business?"

Ahhh…I got that one loud and clear. Lipstick on a pig is still a pig? Needless to say, I did not pursue that lead. Of course, it made all the sense in the world to me, and I had not thought about integrity like that ever before. I was young when this happened and I respected my friend, whom I am still very good friends with some twenty years later. I trusted my friend to make a great judgment call, and to protect me from a potentially bad decision. This brings me to my next point of being of the highest of integrity—trust!

Trust is earned over a period of time, right? Absolutely—it most certainly is! Remember in the first chapter I asked you if you would leave your newborn infant with someone you just met. The answer is still no! That person must be of integrity, but they must also be trusted, too.

Trust is a huge part of being of the highest of integrity. Trust gives you that ability to shake someone's hand knowing full well they will follow through with what they just told you they would do. Trust is having someone tell you, "It's a done deal," and you believe them without hesitation. Trust is one's confidence placed in another human being to do the right thing, to do it honorably, and to do it with the highest of integrity. Trust is being reliable.

Trust is an emotional state for people as it is where you might expose your vulnerabilities to others and having the belief that they will not violate or take advantage of your candor. I trust another person not only because it is in our human nature to do so, but because I have history with you, and I know you to be of high integrity.

Trust is the ability to share information with another, and having faith that what they tell you is factual without misrepresentation. If I buy a car from you, I expect you to be trustworthy in giving me the right information. Am I buying a lemon, or I am getting good value for my money?

Even with the car facts we have today from the internet showing a car's history, you can still get the wool pulled over your eyes. Interestingly enough, you don't hear too many sales people telling you "Don't buy our cars. They are all lemons!" But that is not my point. I should be able to go to anyone and have them tell me straight up if I am getting a great deal or not. And I should believe them because I trust they are "whole" in their values and beliefs.

Your Following

You will gather a following when people know that you have great morals, a great belief system with sound values, and deal with the highest of integrity. People want that in their lives. People need that in their lives. The greatest achievement in anyone's life is when you put all these elements in place together, and they work in tandem with each other. This is what is called creating a great legacy.

Wow, how cool is that? You are now richer than anyone on the planet as you have honor, and people know that your family always dealt with the highest of values, beliefs and had integrity. That beats the snot out of having no integrity, screwing people out of money, having them place no trust in you, cheating on your wife, and having nobody at your funeral, except the director and maybe a priest—if you're lucky.

Having a legacy means that your children and your children's children can walk in anywhere on the face of the earth and have people say, "Ah…there goes the Priakos family. What awesome people they are."

That is what it is all about—plain and simple. I want people to strive to get Principle #3 down and do it consistently. You will have a great following, a wonderful fulfilling life, and a great company of friends that would do anything in the world for you. Isn't that what we all want?

Then why do we complicate things so much? Why do we try to "get away with it?" Why do some people say, "Just do it. Everyone else is doing it." No! Everyone else is not doing it, so stop doing it. I don't care if someone is trying to tell you that it is okay to skim from the top, it is not okay! Never, ever is it okay. You have to be the one that says, "No, that is not right." And they say in turn, "You're not going to tell on me are you?" Just say, "No. It is not my place to tell on you."

We're not in third grade here, but let me ask you this—do you think your actions merit you stealing from the till? I'm just giving you an example here of petty theft, but it is still wrong; and if you ever do that, you will never be of high integrity.

Some years back, I had a boss who was a manager of one of our investment banking firms where people were trading millions and billions of dollars each and every day. One morning he deliberately dropped a crisp "marked" one hundred dollar bill on the hallway floor and walked away quickly. He wanted to test the honesty of his employees, and this was his way of testing us. About 15 minutes later he came back and the crisp new bill had disappeared.

He gave the thief another 30 or so minutes to come clean and turn in the bill to the manager of the office. Still nothing happened. The boss came over to the middle of trading room floor and shouted out to everyone, "Can anyone here please let me borrow a few hundred bucks for lunch. I am taking out a customer and I forgot my wallet at home. I'll pay you back tomorrow."

A few shouted back that they didn't have that much on me—but a select few stepped up and offered to loan the boss a few hundred bucks. We were all making large amounts of money so asking anyone for a hundred or three until the next day was no big deal to us at all.

Of the few standing there, one young intern told him, "I have a hundred to loan you sir." With one glance he spotted the bill with his mark on it. *Ah*, he thought to himself. The thief fell for it. "Where did you get this bill son?" he asked sternly. The intern just shrugged and repeated, "You can have it and pay me back tomorrow."

What balls, the boss thought to himself--*this sonofabitch is stealing my money and wants it back tomorrow to boot.* He glared at him for a moment, then picked his head up, faced the room and shouted loudly. "Attention brokers!" Everyone stopped dead in their tracks. "I want you all to look at Mr. So-and-So here. That's right. I want everyone to take a very good look at him please." And everyone was watching.

He scanned the room looking at everyone while saying, "I just asked you all for a few hundred dollars for lunch, which I do not need. I just wanted you all to see that Mr. So-and-So was kind enough to loan me my own f*$%* money!"

He then turned to the young intern. "You see son, this is my money. See that mark on the back of the bill?" The intern nodded slowly. "I placed that mark on a one hundred dollar bill earlier this morning. It is the exact same bill you offered me just now." The intern was now trembling.

"I should be able to drop this bill on the floor and two things and two things only should occur." You could hear a pin drop on that floor—it was that quiet. The boss continued, "A person should pick it up and bring it to the office manager stating that someone had dropped a hundred dollar bill, or my friend here, Mr. Ben Frickin' Franklin, should stay on the floor all day, with no one bothering him."

You could actually see this young kid start to cry. "Son, we deal with hundreds of millions of dollars at this firm, and if I cannot trust you with one hundred dollars, how the hell can our customers trust you with their money." The young man's body language was slouched, and his head was very low. The boss finally said to him calmly. "You're fired son! Just leave and go to the bottom floor. We will have security escort you and clear out your belongings. You can get them at the front door when they bring it to you."

With this story, I think that you can tell a few things from it. First of all, there are a still few good guys left on Wall Street, and I was proud to work alongside them and call them friends.

I also want you to remember that this same scenario happened in the movie "Trading Places" with Dan Aykroyd and Eddie Murphy—a movie about Wall Street and ethics. If you have not seen the movie, do rent it. It is a classic. Oddly enough, the event in our offices took place a year before the movie came out. I often thought the producers of the movie got the idea of "the stolen bill-fold scene," in the movie, from my boss, but I doubt it.

Now let me tell you what happened to the intern. He could never get a job at any firm and was banned from the business forever. It wasn't because the boss got on the phone to call all the market firms warning them about this person. It was much worse than that.

Every registered investment advisor in the United States fills out two very important forms during their career. When they are hired they fill out a highly detailed form called a Uniform Securities U-4 form. All of us investment bankers/brokers/advisors have to fill out this form, which gives your employer a history of your life and your background. You must fill out "exactly" where you have lived and where you have worked (with no gaps in time) for the last 10 years of your life. Ten years! I can barely remember what I did for my last birthday or what I ate for breakfast this morning!

The other form is the Uniform Securities U-5 form, which is filled out by the compliance department of the firm when you leave, retire or are terminated. The U-5 form also states the reason you were let go, and it follows you throughout your entire career as an investment advisor/securities broker. This poor lad was out of the business before he even got started. No firm would touch him because his U-5 stated he was terminated from his last job for theft.

I felt sorry for the young lad, but not for long. It was a valuable lesson for him to learn, and he learned it the hard way but a lesson nonetheless.

So I will ask you again. Why do people do stupid things and not deal with the highest of integrity? It all boils down to what your belief system and values are. The measure of your success can only be measured by what you have learned in your past.

Some people think that society has done them wrong or they were dealt a bad hand, so to speak. It gives way to contempt and they end up robbers, liars, cheaters; and they steal because someone stole the life they were supposed to have.

Let me be really blunt here and speak first of the stuff that defies logic. Why do some people tell you that they are going to do something and then sit on their big fat…sofa…and then do nothing? I'll give you one better than that. How about when you tell someone that you need to see a doctor or that you wish to meet someone of importance?

The first thing out of their mouth is, "Oh, let me give you my doctor's name. He's the best and you only need to be seeing him." Or they might say to you, "I can get you a meeting with Mr. Big Shot. He's a personal friend of mine." Not only do they "not" know that person, but most times, they don't know who you're talking about.

This stems from the fact that people in their inner desire, on a subconscious level, need to feel important and significant. It is a human element of who we are, and that desire to feel significant can sometimes backfire on us because we are not of the highest integrity.

Some people have an internal struggle with themselves—a conflict if you will—because even though they mean well and their intentions are good, they still try to feel significant and important.

To be of the highest integrity you must do or say what you are going to do all of the time, not just some of the time.

What I mean by this is very simple. When you tell someone you are going to do something then bloody well do it. If you tell your friend that you will look into something for them, then you must do what you said you were going to do. It is just that complicated.

Here's when complications or miscommunications happen. Let's say you have just told your friend, who is in need of a new job, that you know somebody at a particular firm; and you will make a call on his or her behalf. You then tell your friend that you will get back to them right away to tell them what happened. Remember, this person needs a job now! They are turning to you for a lifeline.

If you truly do have a connection and the resources at "ABC" company, then by all means make the call immediately, not tomorrow or next week. Do it now! Not only will it make you feel good about yourself and make you feel significant, but more importantly, you have further established a greater "trust" with your friend because they are counting on you to help them as you stated you would.

That is being of high integrity. You said you were going to do it just as you stated you would. So, you make the call and leave a message for your resource at "ABC" company that your friend is looking for a job, and you would appreciate a call back to point them in the right direction. You then call your friend back and tell him what you just did. This only took out a few minutes out of your busy day, but something more important happened here. You made your friend feel at ease. They turned to you for help, and you were "Johnny-on-the-spot," and took action immediately.

Yes, it is called integrity because you were a person of your word. You did what you said you were going to do and you did it immediately. That my friends are what people will remember about you when you are long gone from this earth.

Whether or not your friend got the job is not important here. What is important is that you took action. You did what you said you were going to do. Your friend thanks you for helping them, and it didn't take you long to do it.

Conversely, let's look at this from the other angle. Your friend calls you up and states that he is looking for a job, and you say that you know someone at "ABC" company; and you will make a call on their behalf. You hang up with your friend and go about your day and never make that call. There are two things at play here. The first one is that you know zero people at "ABC" company, but you wanted to sound important to your friend. You just gave them information that was not only inaccurate but a downright lie.

The second thing at play here is that you do indeed know someone at "ABC" company, but you are taking your sweet time calling them when it is convenient for you. Your priorities shifted to what was convenient for you, not your friend. Again, your friend needs a job fast and turned to you for that lifeline, and you did not make it a priority.

A week goes by and your friend has not heard from you. They ask you if you called "ABC" company for them, and again the same two things come into play here. You either tell that person that the person at "ABC" hasn't gotten back to you (a lie), or you tell them that you forgot to call and you will do it this week for them.

Well, hell, that's no help. Your friend needs as job today, not next week. So you have violated that "trust' with your friend. It's not because you were lazy and didn't make the call, but you did not react with the highest of integrity. You didn't do what you said you would do.

It is these itsy bitsy things that define you as a person my dear readers. These little things may be insignificant to you, but to another person, they are monumental. It is called integrity.

Let's go down the road a few years from now, and that person needs something that is very important to them. They are trying to figure out who they need to call, and as they are sorting through numbers on their phone they come across your number. What do you think that person's first thought to themselves might be?

Naw…I won't bother calling so and so. They never follow through with anything they say they are going to do. That person, scrolling through their phone coming upon your name, doesn't immediately say to themselves, "This person is not of high integrity." But I promise you that their subconscious is telling their brain exactly that.

If you are a person that does what they say they are going to do 100 percent of the time, and you do it to the best of your ability, people will remember that forever. You are consistent with your word, and they can count on you as a person that says and does what you said you were going to do! That is integrity.

You want to be the guy—or gal—that walks into a social gathering and someone introduces you to people and they immediately say, "Oh, you're Ari? It's so nice to meet you. I've heard nothing but great things about you from my friend here." Isn't that a great feeling? It is much better than walking in to that same social gathering, and people don't want to talk to you because they know your history of not being honest or of not being of high integrity. Or they know you are the one that is cheating on your wife, or stole money from the company, or whatever the case may be. Your integrity—or lack thereof—will follow you for the rest of your life, and that is a fact, Jack!

Think of integrity as a seed. When you are young, you have reference points of what is honest and what is not. Your collective consciousness tells you so and gives you the ability to reason for yourself.

How you plant that seed of integrity and water it, nurture it, and watch it grow, will determine how you lead your life either honestly and with integrity, or dishonestly and without moral principles. People will indeed judge you for who you are, not what you are.

The Seed of Integrity

Once, there was a very successful businessman. He was growing old, and he knew it was time to choose a successor to take over the business. Instead of choosing one of his directors or his children, he decided to do something different. He called all the young executives in his company together.

He said, "It is time for me to step down and choose the next CEO. I have decided to choose one of you." The young executives were shocked, but the boss continued, "I am going to give each one of you a seed today – one very special seed. I want you to plant the seed, water it, and come back here one year from today with what you have grown from the seed I have given you. I will then judge the plants that you bring, and the one I choose will be the next CEO."

One man, named Jim, was there that day and he, like the others, received a seed. He went home and excitedly, told his wife the story. She helped him get a pot, soil and compost and he planted the seed. Every day he would water it and watch to see if it had grown. After about three weeks, some of the other executives began to talk about their seeds and the plants that were beginning to grow.

Jim kept checking his seed, but nothing ever grew. Three weeks, four weeks, five weeks went by, still nothing. By now, others were talking about their plants, but Jim didn't have a plant and he felt like a failure.

Six months went by — still nothing in Jim's pot. He just knew he had killed his seed. Everyone else had trees and tall plants, but he had nothing. Jim didn't say anything to his colleagues; however, he just kept watering and fertilizing the soil. He so wanted the seed to grow. A year went by and the CEO asked the young executives to bring their plants to work for inspection. When Jim told his wife that he wasn't going to take an empty pot, she asked him to be honest about what happened. Jim felt sick to his stomach, it was going to be the most embarrassing moment of his life, but he knew his wife was right. He took his empty pot to the board room.

When Jim arrived, he was amazed at the variety of plants grown by the other executives. They were beautiful – in all shapes and sizes. Jim put his empty pot on the floor and many of his colleagues laughed, a few felt sorry for him!

When the CEO arrived, he surveyed the room and greeted his young executives. Jim just tried to hide in the back. "My, what great plants, trees and flowers you have grown," said the CEO. "Today one of you will be appointed the next CEO!

All of a sudden, the CEO spotted Jim at the back of the room with his empty pot. He asked Jim to come to the front of the room. Jim was terrified. He thought, *The CEO knows I'm a failure! Maybe he will have me fired!*

When Jim got to the front, the CEO asked him what had happened to his seed. Jim told him the story. The CEO asked everyone to sit down, except Jim. He looked at Jim, and then announced to the young executives, "Behold your next Chief Executive Officer — Jim!"

Jim couldn't believe it. Jim couldn't even grow his seed. "How could he be the new CEO?" the others said. Then the CEO said, "One year ago today, I gave everyone in this room a seed. I told you to take the seed, plant it, water it, and bring it back to me today. But I gave you all boiled seeds; they were dead – it was not possible for them to grow. "All of you, except Jim, have brought me trees and plants and flowers. When you found that the seed would not grow, you substituted another seed for the one I gave you. Jim was the only one with the courage and honesty to bring me a pot with my seed in it. Therefore, he is the one who will be the new Chief Executive Officer!"

- If you plant honesty, you will reap trust
- If you plant goodness, you will reap friends
- If you plant humility, you will reap greatness
- If you plant perseverance, you will reap contentment
- If you plant consideration, you will reap perspective
- If you plant hard work, you will reap success
- If you plant forgiveness, you will reap reconciliation

*Character is like a tree and reputation
like its shadow.
The shadow is what we think of it;
the tree is the real thing.*

Abraham Lincoln

Principle #4

Always Seek Wisdom

The Atom Smasher

It was one of those cold, rainy days in Los Angeles--I was living in Venice Beach at the time. On any normal day, if you wish to call Venice Beach normal, one would usually see the early morning hustle 'n bustle of people scurrying about doing their morning walk or stroll, roller blading up and down the boardwalk or just casually walking down the beach with their coffee.

The latter were either the surfers gauging the swells of the ocean to catch some "gnarly" early morning waves (especially "choice" for this time of winter) or the retirees walking down the beach leering at the idiots wanting to surf in this kind of weather. Go figure!

But on this particular day, it was just plain wet: wet concrete, wet sand and wet hair everywhere. Just so you know, you just don't see too many Southern Californians with umbrellas or raincoats. People who live in SoCal think the rain is going to stop any minute (when it actually rains), and the streets aren't slick with oil! That's SoCal for you and why I prefer Northern California. Good Lord, now I am going to get letters from my LA friends, so please don't write. I just prefer San Francisco better than LA. Leave me alone already!

As I was saying, it was wet! During this time, I was an investment banker and we were working on significant deals, raising capital from investors to build out the SMR (Specialized Mobile Radio) towers in various parts of the country. This was an arduous task because no one had ever heard of SMR technology back then. To give you an idea, it is the bandwidth in the 800 MHz (megahertz cycle) that is used by today's cell phone carriers. We were not only selling the bandwidth for direct line of sight television towers, but it was also our job was to help fund the build-out of the cell towers and infrastructure from LA to Oxnard, CA. Today, you would know this company as Nextel Communications. But back then, you had to have tremendous vision and an incredible appetite for risk. These investments were not for the timid, that's for sure.

The day's business was on my mind but more importantly, I was starving. I think I had been out late the night before watching turtles race (I'm not joking) and probably had one too many, thus my fuzzy head. I needed some pancakes and greasy bacon for sure!

On the way to the office, and if I had the time, I might usually stop at the Bob's Big Boy on Lincoln Ave. If you don't know about Bob's Big Boy, it is a glorified Denny's, but they're the ones with the ginormous sign statue in the shape of a young boy with huge wavy black hair. He's in a red and white checkerboard apron, and he's hoisting a cheeseburger near his shoulder the size of a small car. So now you know…that's a Bob's Big Boy.

I parked my car, grabbed my umbrella (yes, I owned an umbrella), and scooted into the restaurant as fast as I could without getting soaked to the bone. I was trying to protect my very expensive Armani suit from getting wet. Yeah, I wore very expensive suits.

These days I am more comfortable in my blue jeans and cowboys boots--which is how I go to work every day, and it's also my attire for public speaking engagements. Hell, I want to be comfortable and not looking like I just got off the trading floor of the NYSE for Pete's sake. As I was saying—I walked in the restaurant and grabbed a booth. I'm one of those guys that prefer a booth over a table, if you know what I mean.

It was somewhat quiet in the Bob's. I grabbed a menu, which was pointless as I already knew what I wanted to eat. The waitress came towards me and poured me a hot coffee. She asked me if I needed more time as I was holding on to the menu, looking pathetic and staring at her as if she were going to read off the chef's daily specials.

I ordered my usual hangover special: two eggs (over easy), hash browns, four strips of bacon, two pancakes (with extra syrup on the side), and two pieces of white toast. Yeah, I know what you're thinking. I got enough starch with the pancakes. Yeah, yeah! Shoot me—I like white toast.

As I am waiting for my order, I grabbed the morning WSJ and started perusing the headlines and going over the financial news from yesterday. I kind of figure getting yesterday's news from Wall Street is like waiting for a free beer when the sign above you says, "Free Beer Tomorrow." I chuckle when I see that sign as I like to believe that there is some poor SOB out there who is actually still waiting for his free beer. What's the point!

Waiting for my eggs and pancakes, I noticed an elderly couple walk into the Bob's. Like I said, it wasn't too terribly busy and they had their pick of tables, but for some reason they elected to sit in the booth directly across the aisle from me. *They were so adorable*, I thought to myself. How sweet as the husband made sure his wife got in the booth safely and was comfortable. She removed her plastic hooded raingear, and he took off his jacket and draped it across the head area of the booth. They got situated, and she reached out to hold his hand, which he gently took. It was simply wonderful to see this couple, obviously married for a very long time, still care about each other in that way. It was a very loving scene. The events that unfolded that morning have stuck with me to this very day, some 30 years later.

Isn't that amazing about memories? As I have written before in my books and spoken about in my lectures and in my seminars, memories are something that no one can take away from you. And if you paid attention to Principle #1, making great decisions will indeed give you some pretty awesome memories!

My new soon-to-be-friend in the booth across from me had obviously made a great decision many, many years ago when he married the woman sitting across from him—but I'll get to that in just a wee bit. The memories I have of that particular morning are so strong in the memory bank of my brain, it seemed like it happened just yesterday. I can remember it that well.

I didn't want to stare at them, but they were a ridiculously cute and adorable couple, who were content just enjoying the morning together and being in each other's company. *We should all be so lucky,* I thought.

I returned my attention to my WSJ, sipped on my coffee and minded my own business…kind of. I was fascinated with this couple, and the love that emanated from their table, the joy and merriment. Was something to behold. It is actually hard to put it into writing, but you know what I am talking about. It is a human feeling and emotion that is very hard to describe, but I think you know where I am going with this.

You might be asking yourself about right now, Hey Ari. I thought you said this chapter was on wisdom? Having wisdom is also having a certain degree of patience. Thus, that's your first lesson in wisdom.

Ah...my order has arrived. There are my pancakes, my toast, my eggs, and my bacon. Oops! I forgot to order my orange juice. I kindly asked the waitress for a large orange juice.

"I never start my day without my orange juice!" said the voice close to me. I was puzzled. I turned to my right and to my amazement, the old gentleman had heard that I ordered orange juice; and I'll be a son of a gun--if he wasn't holding up a tall glass of OJ as if toasting to me.

"I agree with you," I replied back to him. *What a nice man,* I thought to myself. I looked again at him, and he was still holding his wife's hand while raising his orange juice to me at the same time. *I had to meet these people,* I said to myself.

"A little wet this morning, don't you think?" I said to engage him in conversation.

He replied, "From where we come from this is normal."

I said, "Really, and where is that, if I may ask?"

"The Midwest," he said.

I responded by telling him that I knew exactly what he was talking about as I spent several years in Chicago. He then introduced himself and his wife as Joe and Sarah (not their real names), and then I told them my name.

"Ah…you're Greek then?" he said to me. "Yes sir, I sure am," I replied. He quickly responded, "I have many dear Greek friends back home, but we lost touch with them when we moved here many years ago. Most of them have passed away though." I told him how sad that was, and he thanked me pleasantly. His wife said very little the whole time that Joe and I chatted away like we were old pals.

He and Sarah were originally from Ohio and moved to California many decades earlier. He didn't tell me exactly when he moved, he just said, "many decades ago." I left it at that. During our conversation I was trying to eat my pancakes and eggs, but the conversation I was having was much more interesting than my cold eggs.

We talked about the differences between living in California as opposed to the Midwest, and the differences in family values from one state to another. In his opinion, they differed greatly. I agreed with him. Not because I was trying to pleasant, but because what he was saying was a fact! I found that I was asking him questions like a student would ask the master. That's exactly what was happening here. I was learning about life from this wonderful person.

There was a brief silence and I looked at him and asked, "Joe, if I may be so bold to inquire, how young a man might you be?" He looked at me and said, "Well Ari, you don't have to be bold to ask a question like that of me, but I appreciate you asking. I am 90 years young and Sarah here is a spritely 88!" Joe truly did not look 90, that's for dang sure. He was of small frame, worn round glasses, hair receded as you might expect for a man of his age, parted on the side; and he had a most wonderful smile. Somewhat contagious if you know what I mean. You could just tell that he had probably worn a smile on his face most of his adult life. He was a man that just enjoyed life, and I'm sure lived it to the fullest.

His suit was the type you might find on your grandfather, and he really looked the part of the perfect American grandfather. Someone you would most certainly see in a Norman Rockwell painting. Sarah, on the other hand, was very well dressed. I think the word I'm looking for here is that she looked "refined." And it was first thing in the morning to boot! She was indeed spritely and an extremely young looking 88.

She looked like she could have been a grade school teacher or something like that. She wore black horn-rimmed glasses, and a very attractive and colorful scarf that graced her neck, with her long snow white hair flowing down to her neckline. She was a very attractive lady for her age. They were just adorable together, and I bet you a buffalo nickel that was the first love of his life.

"Yes sir," Joe continued. "On top of everything else Ari, we just celebrated our 60th wedding anniversary last week.

"Wow! Sixty years together" I shouted. "That is fantastic!" I wanted to know what their secret was, so I asked them. "After 60 years of being together, might either you share with me what the secret is to your nuptial bliss?" Sarah chimed right in and didn't miss a beat. "Lots of wine Ari…lots of wine."

They both chuckled aloud, and then I started to chuckle, which turned into a good laugh. I thought to myself, *how cool is that?* He obviously married his soul mate. After 60 years of marriage it was obvious they did everything together, and loved each dearly since the day they married.

I want you to pay attention to this next part, because it is the first lesson of wisdom. One thing about wisdom that I learned that day is that you must seek it out. You get wisdom by asking questions, by learning from others, and also by trial and error. You can also have your head buried in the sand and go through life without seeking it out and learning the hard way. We call that ignorance.

You may have the greatest nugget of wisdom staring you right in the face, but if you are not receptive to it, you might just miss that nugget. Our elderly are some of the greatest sources of wisdom that we have on the planet, yet we ignore them or sometimes just pass them off for being old.

My mother Penelope, who passed away when I started this book, was a walking book of wisdom. Even I am guilty of not heeding a mother's advice to her son. It was advice that many times I did not pay attention to. I thought that I knew better. I miss her and our talks terribly, but I'll never forget her words of encouragement and her words of wisdom to me.

My father was a highly learned man, extremely intelligent; but he passed away when I was in my 20s so my mother was my guiding light of wisdom. I just didn't listen to her many times. My point is this: Why do we turn our backs on learning from our parents? So if you have parents that truly care for you, for the love of God, listen to them.

Wisdom comes in many forms, which I will get to in just a minute. That morning at Bob's, I learned a very valuable lesson about keeping my ears, my eyes and my brain open to asking the right questions of those that have already blazed a trail in front of us all. Your mind is like a parachute—it doesn't work unless it is open! So open your mind, ears, and eyes to always seek out wisdom.

"Hey, Joe. Can I ask you a question, sir?

"Of course, Ari, and please don't call me sir. Every time someone calls me sir, I look over my shoulder for my father…hee-hee." I thought it was kind of funny as well, so I laughed with him.

"What did you do for a living Joe? I am of the hope that you and your wife are retired, but can you share with me what you did in life?" His answer lit me up!

"I'm a physicist Ari!" he replied.

If you just caught that, Joe didn't say he *was* a physicist. He said he *is* a physicist.

The pitch of my voice was higher as I inquired with the greatest of interest. "You're a physicist?'

"Yes, sir. As a matter of fact, I helped design the Linear Particle Accelerator at Stanford." *Holy crap,* I said to myself. I am sitting here having breakfast with a leader of modern science and a possible Nobel Laureate. Just so you know there are only a few people on the entire planet that have this kind of mind.

The Linear Particle Accelerator built at Stanford University was called "The Monster" for the scientists that helped build it. Its purpose was to accelerate electrons to nearly the speed of light for groundbreaking experiments in creating, identifying and studying subatomic particles.

It really doesn't matter if you have a fundamental understanding of physics or not, the fact of the matter is that I was having breakfast with a legend in his field of science.

"That is amazing, Joe. How much fun was that?" I felt like an idiot after those words left my mouth. Fun? I'm sure it was extremely intense work, applied sciences of so many areas of physics and quantum mechanics. I could not even possibly fathom the years of studying it must have taken to get to this kind of level.

Joe got to a point in his life where he earned the right and was given the chance to participate and work on groundbreaking science. It's a science that would change the world, how we look at the solar system, and where we fit in our own universe. Wow!

"It was a helluva lot of fun," Joe said. I loved his answer and it made me more interested in the next question I was about to ask.

"I have another question for you Joe…if you do not mind."

"Go ahead, Ari. I'm enjoying our conversation."

"Thank you, sir…uh hem…I mean, Joe" remembering that he wanted to be called by his first name.

I don't know what made me ask this next question—it just came to me. Not only was I stunned by his answer, but it was something I never forgot and something I have always asked of people that are in their golden years.

"In all the experiences you have had in your life Joe, what would you say is the single greatest thing, accomplishment, or event that you have witnessed in your 90 years on this earth?

Guess what he said to me. "Ari, my boy. That is the easiest question I have ever been asked?"

While waiting for his answer I anticipated in advance what his answer to my question might be. Surely this man of science thinks that man walking on the moon was the greatest thing he ever saw. How about the invention of the electron microspore or Nanotechnology? No, I thought. He's got to be thinking that the greatest thing he has ever witnessed was the eradication of diseases such as polio? No, that's not it. Well then, it has to be the discovery of the neutron, the pulsar, or the theory of the Big Bang! No certainly not that, although that is pretty big (pun intended)!

I know! It was the theory of the accelerated expansion of our universe or dark matter theorems. Dammit! It's one of those. What seemed like an eternity in my mind was only a millisecond, and then Joe said it so succinctly.

"Witnessing the birth of my first child was the greatest thing that I have ever witnessed in my 90 years on this earth." He held his wife's hand, looked at her and she at him, and then Joe gave her a little wink and squeezed her hand ever so gently and lovingly.

What just happened? Seriously…what the hell just happened? Dammit! That is not the answer I was looking for but wait a minute. Whoa, Nellie! What an amazingly perfect answer. God creates life, man teaches child, child becomes man, man teaches child and God takes man back! How incredibly perfect being the witness of God's miracle. It's the beginning of life!

"Joe, I am stunned, I must say. I sit here humbled by your genius, and I expected a completely different answer than the one you just gave me. But after thinking about it, what a completely beautiful response." I looked over at Sarah. She just smiled and nodded at me slowly with her eyes almost shut. It was like she was thinking about the very day she gave birth. You could see joy in her face.

"You see, Ari, when Sarah was pregnant with our first child, we had midwife's way back when."

"I understand," I responded.

"When you are looking down at the woman who gave birth to your child, and you are holding her hand and you get the chance to be a witness to God's miracle, there is nothing greater in the world than that miracle of birth." I just sat there listening to every word he said.

Joe went on. "You can think about all the science and medicine you want, or going from the horse and buggy to automobiles, or even machines that fly through the air. But, there is no greater event in my life as witnessing my daughter pop her cute little head out and take her first breath of life"

That about put me over the edge. Joe sipped on the last portion of his coffee and indicated to his wife that they needed to go. I just sat there taking it all in. What beautiful people. What a memorable morning. What an incredible answer to one very simple question.

Wisdom Is All Truths In the Universe

You can look no further in all that surrounds you for wisdom is everywhere. For some, they could trip over wisdom and not realize they were directly or indirectly introduced to it. Space, our universe, and the way we look at the mysteries of the world stem from the wisdom of man's sublime conscious thoughts.

My personal religious background is of the Christian faith. I believe in God, the Father Almighty, maker of heaven and earth. Even though I know my Savior is Jesus Christ, it does not preclude the fact that I respect the religious beliefs of others whether it stems from the wisdom of Buddhism, Hinduism, Confucianism, or even Taoism, just to name a few. This chapter is in no way meant to express any particular religious beliefs, but the common denominator of the belief systems of the religions I mention above gives us all tremendous enlightenment and wisdom.

The two questions I have for you are: Do you seek wisdom, and secondly, do you understand it? Seeking out wisdom is one thing. Understanding what you are absorbing in wisdom is something completely different.

I look at Buddhism, which in my opinion, and as others may believe, is beyond a religion. It is about philosophy and a way of life. Oddly enough, the etymology of the word "philosophy" stems from the Greek meaning "love of wisdom."

Enlightened at the age of 35, Siddhartha Gotama, known as Buddha, set forth to seek out wisdom as the key to human happiness. His "awakening" started his teachings of the principles of Buddhism and that "Dhamma" or truth as it is called, was his life's work until his death at the age of 80.

The interesting thing about Buddha was that he never claimed himself to be a God, but a man who taught a path to enlightenment from his own experiences. His wisdom teaches us that we are to be tolerant of other beliefs and religions, and that the concepts of Buddhism can be summed up in the Four Noble Truths and the Noble Eightfold Path.

The first Noble Truth is that life is suffering. Pain, getting old, disease and even death are part of the first noble truth. So are psychological sufferings, such as fear, frustration and disappointment. Buddha's wisdom explained how we can avoid these sufferings and how we can be truly happy. In other words, before you can understand life or death, you must first understand "self." It is the perception you have of yourself, how much value you place in yourself, and how you wish your "self" was really like.

Today's society has placed so much stress on our lives that sometimes we think and feel that the way to happiness is by having great wealth. I know many millionaires that are just plain miserable. Many that do not know that Buddha was born into a royal family and even he, at age 29, realized that wealth and luxury did not guarantee happiness. Keep in mind that this was a little over 500 years before Christ.

Buddha's second Noble Truth explains that we will suffer if we expect others to conform to our own expectations. Buddha explained it as a "craving" in that we, as humans, continually try to seek something else to make us happy, and sometimes no matter how successful we are, we are never satisfied.

That craving is a "want" of something more, and this truth teaches us the wisdom that wanting deprives us of fulfillment and happiness. It goes back to my teachings of needs versus wants. We only need four things to make us truly happy: food, clothing, shelter and love. The rest is all junk; "wanting" a Ferrari or a house on a hilltop on the Amalfi coast of Italy is just stuff and will not make you truly happy.

We go through life trying to attain things that do one thing and one thing only—possession gives us a sense of security about ourselves. It makes us comfortable. We grasp onto material things for dear life to possess things. And, of course, we hold on tight to the concepts, idealisms and opinions we think about ourselves. We truly do think so highly of ourselves, don't we? Unless you have wisdom of "self," you will never truly be happy no matter how much crap you possess.

The third Noble Truth of Buddha is one I really like, as it deals with Nirvana. True peace is something you have within yourself. It is called contentment. However, the third truth deals with overcoming suffering of the first two truths, true happiness comes from giving into useless cravings and wants, and to live each day as it comes.

Dwelling on the past is a suffering all unto itself. If you continue to dwell on what happened in your life, and continue to reflect on it, you will never be truly happy. This is where people get frustrated because in their own world life did not turn out the way it was supposed to, or the way they think it should have turned out, or it simply did not ever meet their expectations.

That type of wisdom also holds true for imagining what the future will bring, which can also be a form of suffering. As I discussed earlier in making great decisions and predicting your future, you have the ability to do so without suffering, but you must first have wisdom of "self."

You live each day in the love and fulfillment that you make of it and that form of happiness, that sense of contentment, will be your nirvana.

The fourth Noble Truth is quite simple actually. It is the Eight-fold Path of being moral. It is what we say to others, how we say it, and how we live our lives. It is the way we think and the way in which we convey our thoughts and emotions towards others. That wisdom is attained by developing compassion for others.

Compassion includes our ability to be sensitive towards others, to share in their feelings and thoughts. Compassion is a willingness to comfort others by offering sympathy and truly caring for another human being. Compassion is understanding the needs of others and to even show mercy to our enemies.

Compassion is an overwhelming sense of care, showing pity and feeling the distress of others' suffering or misfortune. Compassion is ultimately the human desire to help alleviate any pain others may feel.

Buddha's told us that by walking of the path of true "self," wisdom will come from our experiences of truth and reality through the understanding and awareness of your thoughts and actions.

The Wisdom of Consciousness

There is also great wisdom in the teachings of Hinduism, long considered the world's oldest religion as it actually has no beginning. Hinduism precedes recorded history, and it does not have a human founder. Hinduism is somewhat of a mystery, but the basis of the wisdom of Hinduism is that it takes into account the truth "within," and to reach a higher level of consciousness where man and God are one.

The concept of Hinduism and its wisdom is all about a belief system and the outcome of your destiny. Going back to what I discussed earlier in the book, our beliefs determine our thoughts, our actions, and our basic attitude towards life in general. Our actions create direction, and direction will determine our destiny. In Hinduism, this destiny is called Karma. The strong belief in this wisdom, or sometimes lack thereof, is based by the cause and effect, which will ultimately determine your destiny by your actions, your words, and your deeds.

Hinduism beliefs are quite diverse; but first and foremost, they have a strong conviction in a supreme being and endless cycles of creation called reincarnation. Each soul, as they believe, has a destiny and purpose to reincarnate; and wisdom will be attained by the many rebirths until all karmas have been resolved. In other words, you come back until you get it right. I mean this with great respect as reincarnation believes in the wisdom that all karmas need to be resolved, thus a rebirth upon death.

Hindus believe in purification, personal discipline and meditation—to know and be in touch with "self." The belief that all life is sacred is paramount in Hinduism, and life is to be loved and revered.

The great wisdom of Hinduism is in developing your mind to reach "higher self." A person who does not pursue self-knowledge cannot have tranquility. Without tranquility this wisdom teaches us that happiness cannot follow. The person who disciplines their mind will receive tranquility and oneness. Hindu scripture passages state you must keep your mind pure for what a person thinks he becomes.

Certain wisdoms we receive from Hinduism come from the "Puranas," which are sacred Hindu texts eulogizing various deities. The words of the "Garuda" Purana, one of the 18 Puranas, states: "The miserable tend to constantly notice other people's faults. Even if they are as small as a mustard seed; and continuously shut their eyes against their own faults, even if they are as large as a citrus fruit."

As shown in the Garuda Purana, the miserable won't ever seek wisdom for they lack purpose in self-consciousness. They are weak and unaware of wisdom, as lashing out towards others is easy, gutless, and offers no compassion.

How can you reach a level of higher consciousness without first believing and understanding "self" and having the desire to learn and attain wisdom? The answer is: you cannot. Wisdom is the collection of the knowledge in everything that is good and whole. I personally, have never heard of crappy wisdom, have you?

One must purify the mind first and be willing to receive wisdom like an antenna used to receive a signal. If your mind is not trained to receive, you will never get the signal. This unto itself is wisdom, for wisdom carries many textures. Wisdom can also be concealed.

Your conscious mind and your subconscious mind must both be trained to uncover wisdom from the stone it lurks beneath. For when you uncover wisdom, you shall also receive enlightenment.

The Wisdom In Philosophy

At one time or another, we have all met a woman named Sophia. The word "Sophia" comes from the Greek meaning wisdom. Sophia is the wisdom and central idea behind the Hellenic philosophy. I am of Greek descent, born in the United States, but I was constantly surrounded by the Hellenic culture and all that is Greek from my parents.

As a youth, I studied the philosophy of Plato, Socrates, and Aristotle. Many state that some of the greatest minds and philosophers of the world came from Greece. Forget the fact that I am Greek for a moment, okay? I would still have a propensity to agree with the above.

All kidding aside, there are brilliant and wise men from all over the world, but during these ancient times some of the wisest men came from the Class of Athens. Much of the wisdom and philosophy we learned from these scholarly men is still the basis of philosophy study throughout academia.

Socrates was considered one of the wisest men in all of Greece. Many argued that he was not, so to dispel this rumor, a young man was sent to see the Oracle in the city of Delphi, once considered to be the center of the universe. The young man knew the Oracle would have the answer as it was incapable of lying. It was also well-known that the Oracle was a direct connection to the Gods.

The young man arrived in Delphi and asked the Oracle if there was anyone smarter and wiser than Socrates. The Oracle immediately responded and stated without a doubt,

Socrates was indeed the wisest and smartest man in all the land. The young man was startled by this news. *Surely,* he thought to himself, *there must be someone smarter and wiser than Socrates.* Evidently not and as stated, the Oracle was incapable of lying.

So, off the young man went, dashing back into town to find Socrates in the courtyard lecturing to his students. "I have just returned from Delphi and the Oracle told me that Socrates is the wisest and smartest man in all of Greece," the young man declared out loud.

Socrates stopped his lecture and slowly walked over to the young man, now kneeling before him. Socrates looked down into his eyes and said, "My friend. I must be the smartest and wisest man in all of Greece, for I am quite aware of the enormity of my ignorance."

It has been said before, "The dumber you are the smarter you think you are. The smarter you are the more you realize how little you know!" It's simple yet so profound, as Socrates was known to say.

Interestingly enough that during this short time in ancient Greece you had three of the wisest men in all the world teaching us wisdom. Plato studied under Socrates and Aristotle was the protégé of Plato.

All of these men, Socrates, Plato and Aristotle were lovers of wisdom. Plato wrote at length about his teacher's "Socratic" style, which was in the form of dialogue. Question-answer, question-answer, question-answer was the form Socrates used to answer both sides of the question so that he could arrive at a conclusion.

From this wisdom, Plato discovered that mankind is born with knowledge and elaborated that knowledge is present during the time of birth. He stated that it was not so much in the emphasis that you learned things, but that you recollected what you learned later to draw upon your mind's knowledge to reach your own conclusions.

So I'll ask you the following question: If we are born with knowledge, according to Plato, then do we also possess wisdom at birth? I'll let you answer that question with another question. If we have consciousness at birth and we possess knowledge at birth, can we not draw upon that knowledge as a child to draw our own conclusion? How about one more question? Do children have the ability to possess and know wisdom? After what we just discussed and so that you may work the process, I will let you draw your own conclusions. It was always question-answer, question-answer. Thank you, Socrates.

Aristotle was only 18 when he became a student of Plato. What many do not know is that Aristotle started his own school, The Lyceum, and was then the tutor of Alexander the Great.

Aristotle brought us great wisdom from his many philosophies and teachings in the subjects of physics, logic, ethics, music, drama, poetry, zoology and politics, just to name a few. One of the greatest pearls of wisdom was his thinking of universal principles that were derived from experiences. He stated that all experiences, as do his principles, have a starting point, and all principles have a principle. Did I lose you?

Our human experiences are the lifeblood of our lives, and we are all subject to starting points of our memories. Every memory has a starting point, does it not? Of course, it does. So, with certain experiences you may very well also gain wisdom. There are certain moments in your life where you draw on knowledge from your memories.

Therefore, if you are drawing from a memory and you reach a "wise" decision, you have then made your own conclusion based on that new found wisdom. Wisdom is then a collection of a conscious and sometimes a subconscious thought process, based on the information that you process and the knowledge you gain from it.

It was known that Socrates and Aristotle were sometimes declared skeptics. I have a standard running line I use when someone tells me they are a skeptic. I usually say, "That's fine, but it doesn't pay much, does it?" When Socrates declared that he was the wisest man in the land because he knew nothing, he didn't mean to say that his wisdom was the same as being ignorant. More importantly, his skepticism towards himself gave him the freedom and ability to receive true wisdom as an insight or an inspiration.

Let me repeat this. Socrates knew that a man with wisdom should be the first to declare that he knows very little. Conversely, he also knew that he was smart enough to realize and understand that man, in his infinite search to uncover wisdom, had the ability to think freely for himself, without prejudice, to receive true wisdom as insight or inspiration.

How often do we feel that a child should follow a father's example and not his advice? Think about that for a moment. Earlier I asked you a question if a child has the ability to understand wisdom, remember? Children will do what you do and may not necessarily follow your advice.

Children will intently watch their parents' actions, their mannerisms, their speech, their daily routines, and the way they interact and socialize with others. So, children do indeed have the ability to achieve wisdom.

Achieving or gaining wisdom works in concert with inspiration, time, and experience. The longer the time, the more inspiration and experience you will develop. The more inspiration and experience, the greater collection of wisdom is realized.

Wisdom is also used when attempting a task that requires a skill. A wise man uses his knowledge to evaluate a situation, utilize the various options before him, plans which task will be of optimum efficiency, and then executes the plan to yield the best results. When this application is used he achieves the perfect solution and outcome. Remember Principle #1, Make Great Decisions? Wisdom should always come into play when making a great decision as you now have the knowledge, experience, and inspiration to execute that decision to then yield the best result. That result should be a perfect solution and/or outcome.

Wisdom of The Universe

I ponder the great wisdom in the writings of Confucianism and Taoism. They both are of Chinese origin. Confucianism visits temples to pay homage to Ti'en (God or Heaven) where Taoists visit shrines to pay homage to deities like Tai Chi.

Both, however, are ancient styles of living. While the wisdom in Confucianism connects itself with the social aspect and the morality of life, the Taoism core wisdom is focused on the individual and spiritual side of life.

Chinese thought and wisdom is clearly defined by the consciousness of man's close relationship with nature, time, and the universe. The word Taoism or "Tao" means path or road. If you take the path or "the way" of Tao, you are on the road with nature and the life force flowing through all life. This wisdom is to be in harmony with nature.

You have heard the expression, "stop and smell the roses." So to be in Tao and one with nature, you not only smell the roses, but you touch and feel the earth from where the flower grows.

You are one with the wind, the sun, and the fragrance of the earth. This wisdom teaches us that if you are reverent with the earth, it will surrender to you harmony and balance in your life. As it is stated by the founder of Taoism, Lao Tzu, "Being one with nature, he is in accord with the Tao. Being in accord of the Tao, he is everlasting."

Chinese wisdom is a wonderful study of nature, the universe, the spirit, and humanity that is all wrapped in a cloak of knowledge.

Within Lies Wisdom

A wise man thinks of life in stages. The wise man will take the necessary steps and precautions by looking far in advance and predicting what will occur a few steps ahead of everyone else. He thinks first and acts later.

A wise man will always focus his thoughts and actions on whatever the target may be, and he never allows outside interference to stray him from his goal.

A wise man never occupies his mind with negativity and unnecessary thoughts that have no value or purpose. When negativity enters in his thoughts, he knows the root of evil from which it stems.

A wise man takes solace in the positive energy that surrounds him, and he glorifies the light of being one with the universe.

A wise man will look deep into his past, and he will use that as a reference point to draw upon a sensible and wise conclusion from his previous experiences. Past lessons learned will yield a fulfilling and bright future.

A wise man is tolerant and has patience towards others. For this virtue strengthens leadership amongst men.

A wise man listens more than he speaks. It is the fool who will jump to an irrational conclusion without first using his mind to absorb his surroundings.

A wise man seeks out knowledge to further develop his mind, and knows that all new found knowledge has purpose and beauty in everything that is good.

A wise man is understanding with his spouse, for it is he that is the leader and must lead with wisdom to fortify his house. A strong foundation will never crumble or perish, and wisdom will help build it true and strong.

A wise man stares fear in the eyes as his past experience helps calm savagery and nourish courage.

A wise man's tongue will deliver forth pure and true speech. It is the fool whose tongue is sharp and course and wisdom will divulge the stooge.

A wise man thinks freely with no boundaries. His thoughts and his ideas are limitless and have no borders. He is what he thinks, and he thinks what is what.

A wise man is genuine and true to himself and to others. He carries the wisdom of integrity while a fool carries an empty sack of dishonesty.

A wise man masters his abilities and strengthens upon his weaknesses. And it is wisdom that allows us to recognize our inadequacies and hone our skills for improvement.

A wise man gives back to the Earth. As a tree is chopped, it shall be restored with seed.

A wise man gives much of himself and asks nor expects anything in return. Wisdom dictates your reward and is measured by your ability to give unreservedly.

A wise man comforts with his heart as his wisdom will bait the pain from the suffering.

*"Knowing yourself is the
beginning of all wisdom."*

Aristotle

Principle #5

Remove Everything Negative

One of the great success coaches I studied over the years was Jim Rohn (rest in peace), and he tells a great story about the frog and the scorpion. It goes something like this:

It was a rainy day and a frog stood by the bank of the river's edge ready to jump in so he could swim across to the other side. Just as he was ready to jump, out from the woods came a scorpion. The scorpion moved closer and closer to the frog.

"Wait!" said the scorpion. "Don't jump in just yet."

The terrified frog saw the face of death moving towards him. Once again the scorpion said, "Wait Mr. Frog. I wish to get to the other side of the river, just like you, but as you can see, I am a scorpion, and scorpions cannot swim."

"I realize that Mr. Scorpion," the frog stated emphatically. "If you are unable to swim, then how will you get to the other side of the river?"

The scorpion replied, "I was hoping that I could catch a ride on your back."

The frog replied, "Oh no! For you are a scorpion and I see the razor-sharp poison tip at the end of your tail. We would get halfway across the river and you will sting me for sure and then I will die!"

"Oh, no I won't," promised the scorpion. "Think about it for a moment. If I hop on your back and I sting you halfway across the river, we will both perish." After thinking about it for a few seconds the frog said, "That makes sense. Okay, hop on." The scorpion jumped on the frog's back and off they went into the water. The frog never carried a scorpion on his back before, but when he looked up, the scorpion seemed quite content with the safe ride across the river. The frog pushed on.

Halfway across the river, sure enough, the scorpion started stinging the frog. "Ow! No! Stop stinging me! That hurts and I will die. Why are you stinging me? I knew you couldn't be trusted. Why did you do this?" said the frog.

"Because I am a scorpion!!!"

Someone, perhaps maybe even one of your close friends reading this fable would say to you, "That's a cute story, but letting in a little negativity surely can't hurt." NO! NO! NO! Allowing in *any* negativity whatsoever starts the process! It is critical that this sinks in my dear readers.

I am now going to give you one of my own personal quotes. I would like for you to repeat it several times so that it registers deep into your subconscious.

"Negativity is the darkest and greatest invisible force in the universe. The most powerful force is your own mind's ability to change it to a positive immediately."

How Negativity Affects Your Life

Each and every day of our lives we are bombarded with negativity. Negativity at work, your social environment, and even your own family can have a negative impact on your mind-set which, in turn, alters the direction of your thoughts.

Many of the people I coach and train have been blasted with negative comments from their past, so much so that they end up believing it. They were told at a young age that were not good enough, not smart enough, or not pretty enough. That type of negative repetition into your subconscious will result in a negative belief system. Therefore, you stand a higher chance of never amounting to anything, and you will then consider yourself a failure. If you believe it, you will live it.

Is that how some of you perceive yourself? Unfortunately, some of you reading this, this is exactly how you feel and how you see yourself. Henceforth, I want you to stop doing that!

I want you to remember what I am about to tell you as it is so germane to this chapter you cannot help but absorb my next phrase. "Your thoughts live forever!" Repeat that again to yourself three times so it sinks in. Positive or negative thoughts will live forever. As I stated earlier in the book, powerful thoughts will create powerful memories that you will take to your grave. So the question I ask you is this: What are you feeding your brain?

If you feed your brain positive thoughts, it will create positive ripples your life. Feed your brain negative thoughts and disaster is sure to follow. So why do we gravitate to the negative? That answer is because it is easier to dwell on the negative and harder to rewire your brain to think great thoughts. Positive or negative, both will affect your life. By the end of this chapter, my goal is to help you understand that it is not that hard to rewire your mind-set to the positive.

Remember what I just told you…your thoughts live forever. I am going to give you the tools you need to change your mind-set. Once that changes, you will have new memories, a new belief system, and a new set of thoughts that will last a lifetime.

Negativity is also sometimes based on fear. The fear of success, the fear of not being good enough, or here is the best one…the fear people have when they say, "Gee, I dunno. What will my friends think?" Here is a clue for you. Your friends—they already think! Who cares what your friends think. That is a statement not a question, just so you know. Most of the time it is negative thinking or negative actions that will get your mind-set into conflict. Remember, this is your life and nobody, but nobody is equipped nor qualified to tell you how to live it, especially your friends!

I look at a few famous people today who were told negative things early in their life. Did you know that Joel Osteen, famous pastor of Lakewood Church in Houston, Texas, was told early in his career that he would not do very well as a pastor? People told him he would never be as good as his father.

Had Joel Osteen allowed that type of negativity to sink into his subconscious, and believed it, who knows where Lakewood Church would be today. Would there even be a Lakewood Church today? My point is he had a vision for his church and a life that was better than the one others perceived.

I love what Joel Osteen says about negativity. He states, "You're going to go through tough times—that's life. But I say, nothing happens to you, it happens for you! See the positive in negative events."

It is your perception of who you are that stems from the belief system that you tell your brain. Bad thoughts equal negativity. Good thoughts and actions will always conquer evil! So don't allow the scorpions close enough to sting you.

Some people walk around with blinders on so they never see the positive in negative situations. As an example, your numbers at work could be down. Profits are not as good as they were the month or the year before. Instead of dwelling on the negative and what went wrong, think of the positive. A positive thought is a signal that you need to tune in to. Remember what I said earlier in the book about direction? Taking action will always create a direction with either positive or negative results. It just depends on what action you took that determines the outcome.

What about negativity in a relationship? The same thing occurs. If you have a partner that is constantly negative, what are your chances of having a lasting and loving relationship with that person? Slim to zero would be the answer. The direction you take in your relationship will most certainly determine a positive or negative outcome, would you not agree? Let's discuss this at a deeper but much simpler level, shall we?

Think of your brain as the bridge of a ship. That is your conscious mind. You can either tell your brain to stay the course in safe waters, or you can change the direction of the ship, head the wrong way where you may very well run aground. On your ship, you have an engine room. The engine room is your subconscious. The men in the engine room have no idea what direction you're going in. The only thing they know is what you tell them to do.

Your brain is also in charge of your mind-set. You can gravitate to the negative and tell yourself how bad your life sucks, or you can overcome every obstacle by thinking positively. In a wee bit, I'm going to show you how to do it.

Solutions to problems absolutely never come out of anyone thinking negatively. Solutions to problems come out of your mind's ability to think positively to then discover ways to overcome those obstacles to get to a solution. Pretty cool, huh? Then why don't we do it? Because you're not giving the engine room the right instructions to tell the bridge your conscious mind!

To see if you are already on a course of running your ship aground, here is a little quiz for you. Answer the following questions as honestly as you can. If you are not completely honest with yourself when answering, then you are cheating yourself out of changing your mind-set, and you will continue to think and do things negatively.

- Do you often think about how crappy your life is? The real question here is: Do you find yourself thinking about it all the time?
- Do you often find yourself complaining about your boss and your co-workers to your friends?
- Do you allow other people's drama in your life? Your best friend's other lady-friend is having an affair with her married boss. Your best friend is now torn between giving her friend advice because at the same time she also has affection for that same boss? Can you stay away from that kind of negative drama?
- Do you criticize, reprimand, or bash people often?
- Do you have a propensity to listen to idle gossip and then make it your business to tell the world about someone else's problems?
- Do you play the victim and feel that people are going out of their way to make your life miserable?
- Do you feel that you are never in control of your own destiny?

- Do you whine and complain to others even when things are going your way?

These are just some examples of the way negativity can affect you. If you answered yes to any of the above questions, your life is being ruled and dominated by negative energy. Your engine room is getting the wrong signals, and your ship is already aground.

By being honest with yourself and answering these questions, you now know what you need to be telling the engine room so the skipper of the ship (you) doesn't run your ship aground. The ship in this example--that's right you guessed it--is your life!

Conversely, positive people, even when things do not go according to plan, find a way to get what they want out of life. They take stock and responsibility for their actions, and they never blame others for the things they do not have. Positive people just make stuff happen because they remove every negative roadblock and obstacle that they encounter.

There are three types of people. Those that make it happen, those that watch it happen, and those that say, "What the hell just happened?" Make sure you are the one who makes things happen, so you steer your ship in the right direction. I find people quite fascinating. On one hand, they might completely realize that they are dwelling on the negative. Yet on the other hand, even after realizing the problem, the first thing they do is try to figure out who is responsible for their misery.

How The Brain Processes Negativity

As you are probably aware, your brain processes information at lightning speed. But what you may not know is that your brain requires more capacity to store negative information than it does positive information? I bet you didn't know that did you? That's okay…most people don't. But why is that, you ask? Without giving you the scientific version, it works something like this.

Your brain and your mind focus on miserable things and negativity more than they do positive. It is just the way your brain works and the way it is wired. Our senses are heightened to watch for danger and obstacles that may be in our path. It also it looks for, hunts out, and searches for negative situations just like a bloodhound on a foxhunt.

Your brain is also trained to pay more attention to negative experiences because negative experiences, and negative events in your life, present an element of danger. Yes, I could very well be talking about a steep, winding road up a mountain. One part of the brain is looking for falling rocks and another part of your brain is watching the road and paying attention to the elements. I am also talking about the way your brain processes negative feedback. We have all experienced negative feedback, either from work or in some kind of social setting.

This is why you must make a hard effort to rewire your brain to see positively instead of negatively. Yes, I still want you to watch the road for falling debris, but I also want you to pay attention to those around you who constantly make negative comments. Those kind of people are a type of debris on your road of life, which must be avoided at all cost. If you don't know what signals to look for, you will run into the boulders that will tumble down from the mountain to hurt you.

You know who they are, and you know exactly the type of people to which I refer. These are the people in your life that hate the environment, hate their boss, hate their marriage, hate the people they work with, can't stand their next-door neighbors, can't stand the person they are in a relationship with; they complain constantly about their ailments. They are never happy about themselves, and so on and so forth.

These could very well be the same people that may have hurt you at some point in your past or are hurting you and holding you back in the present. These are the people that told you that your idea was just that...an idea, and you'd never be able to pull it off. These are the people that told you that you were a failure, or said to that you were not qualified to get that job.

These are the people that told you that you would never make it out of the hood, and you would never make it on your own without their help. These are the people that told you right to your face that you were stupid. These are the people that told you that you destroy everything and everyone you go near. These are the people that made you feel that you were unworthy of their love or that told you no one would ever love you.

Let me ask you this—are "these people" your parents, your guardians or any of your relatives? Are "these people" the ones you trusted or depended on for advice at some point in your life? Are they your friends? Enough already you say! It hurts, doesn't it? I want it to. Not because I want to see any of you in pain. I don't like seeing anyone in pain. What I am after here is that you put yourself in a place where you feel the pain of negative energy. Feeling the deep pain of this negativity is the first step towards changing your mindset, and ridding yourself of the rubbish that steers your ship.

I'm trying to get you to understand how your brain processes this nonsense. Feeling this negative energy first, in its roughest and purest form, is the quickest way to give you a point of reference. A point of reference for what we are about to explore together in getting your mind pointed in a positive direction.

Conquering the nemesis named negativity will give you the ability to give you the ultimate gift. The gift of leading life the way you always dreamed, and it will give you the power to thwart off all the evil in the universe we call dark energy. I'll get back to how your brain processes negativity in a minute, but for now I have another thought I wish to share with you.

We are an odd sort, aren't we? We freely allow this crap in our brain which in turn, adversely affects our lives. Why do we do this? It's because we gravitate towards things like this that many of us can relate to it. We can commiserate with these people because we have lived like that before or worse: it is the way we currently live our lives.

Remember the expression "misery loves company"? Miserable people gravitate towards other miserable people. The interesting thing is that the next thing you know, they are comparing notes as to which one is more miserable. It's like a contest with them. My problems are bigger than your problems, they may say. Oh no, they're not. My issues are much bigger than yours. Oh, woe is me!

I am certainly not telling you to not be a friend or not to have a sympathetic ear. That's not the point. The point is you have to be the stronger one. Lend support to your friend, but then tell them, "I am here for you, but if you want to get rid of your problems then you need to change the way you think first!"

Some people don't want to listen to good advice. They actually want others to confirm their feeling of why they are depressed or have anxiety issues. But one of the most fascinating things I realized about people is that you don't hear too many of your friends saying, "Gee, I understand why you are so depressed. I think you should stay that way for the rest of your life." People never say that, do they?

The Emotional Kill Cycle

Your brain, specifically your subconscious, doesn't know if you are telling it the truth or if you are joking. Your subconscious isn't that smart. It just goes along for the ride, and it will do what you tell it or program it to do. If you tell your subconscious to do something negative, you will keep doing it over and over again. I call this concept "The Emotional Kill Cycle." Let's look at the diagram on the next page.

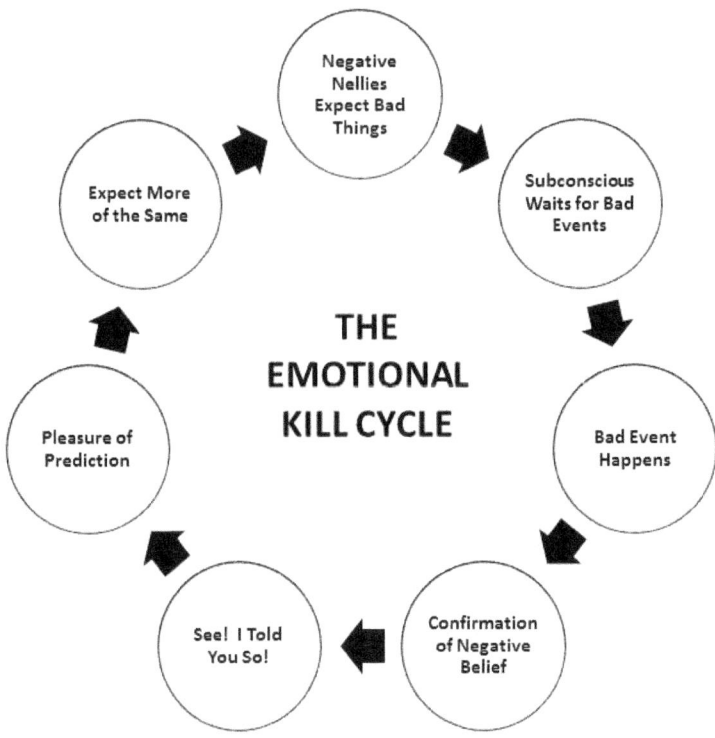

I developed this concept to illustrate how the mind works with negative input into your brain. The Negative Nellies, as I call them, can either be your friends, your social acquaintances, or perhaps even your own family. Anybody reading this book knows someone that is a Negative Nellie.

In my illustration above, starting from the 12 o'clock position, Negative Nellies expect bad things to happen automatically. They don't know any differently so their subconscious expects those bad things to occur. Why, you ask? Your brain works in thought patterns. During the phase right before a bad event, your subconscious is actually looking at the reality of any situation is a negative manner. You've programmed it that way.

This is the point in the Emotional Kill Cycle where people convince themselves that their life sucks, they will never get ahead in life, they can't trust anyone, it is too hard to make more money, and the kicker…great stuff only happens to other people, not to them!

Then, POW! In the next phase, the bad event happens, and they are not surprised in the least. They expect it to happen. I call this part, "The Confirmation Phase."

The next phase right after the Confirmation Phase happens extremely fast and something very interesting occurs. The Negative Nellies experience a sense of euphoria as the brain chemicals, oxytocin and serotonin, kick into overdrive. This starts the "See…I told you so," phase.

The Negative Nellies actually take pride and pleasure of their successful ability to predict the future. They feel good about themselves. This sense of euphoria catapults into the next phase I call, "The Pleasure of Prediction."

It's like the "See…I told you so," walks around with a crystal ball in their hip pocket. For example, you may tell a Negative Nellie you have a great idea for something, like a new invention. They will immediately turn to you and say, "Oh, that's never going to work. I can tell you right now that you're going to fail!" And people actually listen to crap like that and then guess what they do? They won't even implement their idea, and they will quit even before they get started.

The "See…I told you so's," have trained their brain, from repetition, to *expect* something bad to happen; and when something bad actually happens, they aren't surprised in the least. It is expected in their lives. Here is the other sad truth—if someone expects something bad to happen and it turns out good for them, the first thing they say is, "Well, would you look at that. I certainly wasn't expecting that to happen. That won't last long."

Seriously? Of course, it won't last long because now you expect something or someone to take it away from you. The Negative Nellies then wait for the next shoe to drop, thus the cycle continues. That is The Emotional Kill Cycle. Do you know anyone like that? More importantly, and be brutally honest with yourself here, are you like that? Are you a Negative Nellie?

But then you might turn to me and say, "But Ari, it's been like this my entire life. It's always the same. Nothing ever changes for me." Of course it is always the same because you command it to be that way. You've never changed anything different in your life; therefore, your subconscious has no other reference point other than how you program it.

The negative decisions you made two or three years ago affect your life today. If you continue to make the same negative comments, what do you think tomorrow will look like for you? I'm not even going to answer that one.

What about expecting and waiting for something to go wrong right after something positive lands right in your lap? If that is the way you wish to lead your life, or it is the way your life looks like right now, then you will always be miserable.

What's worse is you will always be looking for other miserable people to hang out with who are also trapped in The Emotional Kill Cycle. Misery not only loves company, but misery especially loves The Emotional Kill Cycle. I want this next sentence to sink in really deep. "Negative people have dedicated and invested a helluva lot of time in being negative." It's almost like a job for them. It's like their life's work to get you down and beat you up so they can feel good about themselves.

A truly negative person is always looking for that danger sign because he knows it always looms right around the next corner. Remember, that is how he has trained his brain. He sees the sign that says "Shallow Water. Steer Away!" But they never do change the direction of their ship, even after the warning.

The positive person is already aware of the danger sign, not because he is deliberately looking for it, but because he knows the waters. After seeing the sign far in advance, he takes immediate steps to remove himself from that danger; thereby, steering his ship to safety.

It's not that the positive person is any smarter than the negative person. The positive person just talks to his brain differently, and his engine room responds accordingly. The positive person is not in the Emotional Kill Cycle because he has trained his mind to find a way, and to find a solution, no matter what.

Now that you know some of the signs of negativity and hopefully answered the questions honestly in the beginning of this chapter, you should now know the signals to look out for. But hold on a minute. You say to me, "Hey Ari, I already knew what to look out for. This is simple to understand!" Well, if it is so stinking simple genius, then why do you still allow negativity in your life?

Ah…you don't know how to get rid of it you say? Nonsense! It's a choice my dear readers. You either enjoy being miserable, which I hope is not the case, or you truly want and desire more out of your life. So now *choose* to rid yourself of all the dark invisible forces around you called negativity. Again, it is your choice and one of the greatest acts of freedom we have is of self-worth. You cannot have self-worth if you are negative. Not now, not ever!

With that being said, let us keep exploring how your brain processes negative energy. Later, I will provide you with the emotional tools so you are equipped to obliterate and destroy all the negative cycle patterns in your life, once and for all. The Emotional Kill Cycle will be a thing in your past.

Your Emotions And Negativity

Emotions can be negative just as easily as they can be loving and positive. Have you ever had a negative emotion? Of course you have. We all have. How about the feeling of not having any love in your life? It is a fact that some people who dwell on the negative do not ever see themselves in a relationship because they don't think that anyone will ever love them. Or they feel unworthy of the love from another person.

The next thing their brain does is to create images in their subconscious, and they see themselves alone the rest of their lives. The emotional tug-of-war they have with themselves, and the major conflict, is that they see themselves meeting someone special; but they already know they will most certainly find a way to screw it up. They get into a pattern and repeat it over and over again.

The Emotional Kill Cycle is any emotional pattern the conscious mind can positively create, but the negative embedded in the subconscious is poised and standing by, trained to destroy it.

A person can start off with a positive, loving emotion on a conscious level, but they end up with an Emotional Kill Cycle. Why? Because no matter how positive the emotion is for someone, it is only temporary. The engine room already knows the outcome. It is trained to kill a positive emotional attachment. "Uh oh! Here we go again. We're running aground. Quick everyone, brace yourself for impact!"

What has happened here is that someone who truly wants a healthy relationship has already talked themselves into failure by thinking negative thoughts, which creates negative energy. That negative energy is never a good ingredient for a healthy relationship.

Everyone knows someone that has jumped into a relationship only to find out they are with someone new a month later. A few months after that, they are with someone else. You ask them what happened and they say to you, "Oh, it was doomed from the start. I knew I would find a way to screw it up!" That is an example of an Emotional Kill Cycle.

Another example is when you are involved with another person, and the relationship starts out great. The first few weeks, or perhaps months, are blissful. However, your mindset is not healthy, and you start to revert back to your past experiences and failures. Your subconscious is already programmed for defeat. What happens next is brutal.

You may find yourself putting the other person down. Do you cut the other person off without listening to them? Do you belittle the other person? Have your ever undermined your partner at any time? I saved the best for last—have you ever used negative and hurtful words to another person like, "I wish I never met you." Or, in a fit of anger said, "I hate you!" Ouch! It hurts, doesn't it? These are all examples of the Emotional Kill Cycle. Are any one of you, reading this chapter, saying to yourself, "Bloody hell, Ari…you are describing my life." Well then, let's fix it before it is too late, okay?

Your brain has created even more images of failure. How can any relationship survive that? It cannot. Unless, of course, you change your mind-set and start reprogramming your brain to think positively. It is not as hard as you think, but it does require practice. It's just like anything else you may have done in your life that required repetition, like learning to ride a bike or playing the piano.

You are going to have to learn how to re-condition your thinking from many years of abuse. You are going to learn how to tell the men in the engine room that you are in charge, you're setting a new course and you will need more power to get there. The power in this case is a "shift" in your thinking. Positive thinking requires a powerful technique to shift your mind-set.

A key element I wish for you to capture here is that your emotions are interconnected to your body, although they cannot be visibly seen. This is why I call negativity the most powerful, destructive and "invisible" force in the universe. Your body and mind should work as one, but oftentimes we have internal conflict; therefore, mind and body cannot work in harmony with one another.

Let me give you an example. If your body is releasing chemicals such as endorphins, serotonin or oxytocin, you should be in a state of happiness and euphoria. Conversely, if you are feeling down, depressed and negative all the time, your body is probably releasing cortisol. Once released, cortisol can be the culprit for stirring up depression and anxiety. It is also the monster that can hurt relationships, give you lack of self-esteem and over a long period of time, it can generally be bad for your health.

Yes, cortisol has its place in your body like helping with allergies, for example. But overall, cortisol is a very potent chemical. In high doses, it can cause your body to lower its immune system, gradually retard your thinking, and weaken your muscle tissue, just to name a few.

"All this from being negative?" you ask. Yes! This is why I said to you earlier that allowing just a wee bit of negativity in starts the process. Now you know what the results are to your emotional well-being, and where the path of negativity may lead you--right to the Emotional Kill Cycle.

Let me give you yet another example of the Emotional Kill Cycle. Let's say I were to put you inside an MRI machine to scan your brain. In case you don't know what an MRI is, it stands for Magnetic Resonance Imaging. It's a huge magnetic scanner used in hospitals and clinics to scan your body and your organs to get radio waves to make images. In this case, we would be scanning your brain seeing what your neurotransmitters are doing.

If you were to lie in this machine and I showed you a series of pictures with the word "NO" on it, even for just a second, those monster chemicals will come out and rear their ugly head. Your brain doesn't like the word NO! Even the dolts in the engine room, your subconscious, take refuge when they see words like that.

If your brain doesn't like it, then how do you think the person on the other end of that "NO" feels? Remember the old saying, "Choose your words carefully!" This is very true when you speak to others, as when words leave your lips, they can never be retracted. Have you ever said something to someone that you regretted it right after you said it? The little voice inside your head immediately says, "Boy, I wish I hadn't said that." Well, guess what? It's too late!

Now you have projected negativity onto someone else's well-being because words sting like a scorpion. The sad thing is that those words can leave a negative mental picture in someone else's mind, just as they can leave a life-long impression in your brain.

When you vocalize negativity internally or towards others, the stress chemicals I spoke of earlier actually damage certain emotions. The brain is telling your mouth to say something, but your subconscious is telling you something else altogether. And the pattern is then repeated. Ah yes…yet another example of the Emotional Kill Cycle. Please remember this; the more you engage in negative speech the harder it is to disengage. When you spew out words when your angry and don't mean them, you could very well start acting irrationally.

So, it's not just the word "NO" that makes the brain go nuts, it's a whole bunch of words that have negative connotations that make the chemicals go goofy.

Conversely, the word "YES" is very powerful to anyone's emotional state and well-being, isn't it? Everyone loves to hear the word YES! I would imagine that when a man asks a woman to marry him that word alone sends him into a state of euphoria. All the good chemicals explode inside his head and body. This is equally said for a woman when she utters those blissful words, "Yes, I will marry you!" How cool is that!

When you say "yes" to a job, "yes" to a purchase order, or "yes" to your partner--even when she asks you if you put the dishes away—that three-letter word is pure magic!

Breaking the Cycle of Negativity

Okay. We're getting into my favorite part and that is how do you break this vicious cycle? Just in this chapter, we have uncovered how your brain takes in and processes negativity, and how it can destroy your mind-set and screw with your emotions.

You've read about how being negative can affect your work, your relationships, and more importantly, your health. You even answered my questions, honestly I trust, to see if you are a person whose mind-set thinks negatively on a conscious and a subconscious level. And, you heard the words "Emotional Kill Cycle" for the first time. So...are you ready to crack the code and find out what you can do to shift your mind-set to start thinking positively? I certainly hope so.

What I am about to share with you will require a wee bit of effort on your part, and it requires positive repetition. Many people who think negatively don't actually realize they do it, or don't want to "admit" to themselves they do it. One reason is because they have been doing it for so many years and developed bad patterns and habits. As I said earlier, it is just natural to gravitate to the negative.

In order to break these bad habits, you are going to need to repeat the process I am about ready to teach you. You should do this every single time you feel negativity creeping into your life or mind-set. You have to make this promise to yourself. Here we go.

Have you ever heard of Neural Linguistic Programming or NLP as it is referred? Probably not. To understand what NLP is, let's break it down first.

Neural: Is your brain and your neurological system.

Linguistic: Is the language that your brain receives.

Programming: Is how your brain is being programmed.

Basically, NLP is how we code the language to talk to our brain. You just got the nickel version.

NLP is a very fine science in cognitive psychology and was created by two pioneers in the early 1970s named Richard Bandler and John Grinder. Thousands of books have been written on the subject from their keen research on the study of how the brain behaves one way externally, and then how you process information and behave internally and then outward again.

NLP is also based on a pattern of thoughts and how we think, make decisions, learn so many things, how we process and evaluate situations and events; and more importantly, how our brain learns good and bad habits. With a few NLP techniques I am about ready to teach you, you will have the ability to re-code your thinking process so you can get the results you desire to only think positively from here on out. Let us begin!

The Bull's-Eye Targets of Conflict and Desire

Everyone knows what a target looks like. And everyone knows what you need to do to win. Hit the bull's-eye! That's what we are going to do here. When I do this in public during my workshops and seminars, the process is pretty amazing, and the results happen for people rather quickly.

First, I want you to create a mental image in your mind of a target. It matters not if you have ever played darts or actually been on a target range and held a bow and arrow in your hand before. I just want you to create a target in your mind.

I want this target engrained in your head in the greatest of detail. Is it black and white? Does it have colors like red and white or yellow and black? Are there just two colors or are there multiple colors? Do they alternate colors? One circle being red and the next circle white, then the next one red again? How many circles are there on your target? Fixate this in your head. Don't let any detail go unnoticed.

I want you to be extremely specific on your target. If you played darts in a bar or if you shot a bow and arrow outside, was there any smell associated with that day you played darts or were on the target range?

Take in the smell, if any, and remember what it smelled like that day. Capture that smell of the day in your head. Let it sink in and absorb it all. If your target is outdoors, what is the weather like? Is it a clear day, is it cloudy, or is it raining? Be very, very specific.

Next, I want you to identify if you hear anything? Are birds chirping in the background? Can you hear rain? Whatever image you have of this day and your target, I want you to create this image so it is crystal clear. You are going to want to make this so special it can be recalled at any time, on any given day for the rest of your life.

Okay…if you have that image in your head, great! Now I want you to give it a size. We all know that a bull's-eye target is a circle. If you see your target as a square, then so be it. What the heck, it's your target; it can be whatever shape you wish. Is your target big or small? When you view your target in your mind is it smack dead in front of you or on any one side like to your left or to your right?

Is it big enough that you could physically reach out and touch it or is it off in the distance somewhere? If it is off in the distance, I want you to mentally project it to be closer to you…as close as you wish without it physically touching you.

Now close your eyes as you could not do this before and read at the same time. I want this image of your target as detailed as I just described and as detailed as you have just created it in your mind. Do you see it? Can you count the circles? Do you see all the rings and all the colors? Do you smell the day and know what the weather is like? Got it? Okay, great!

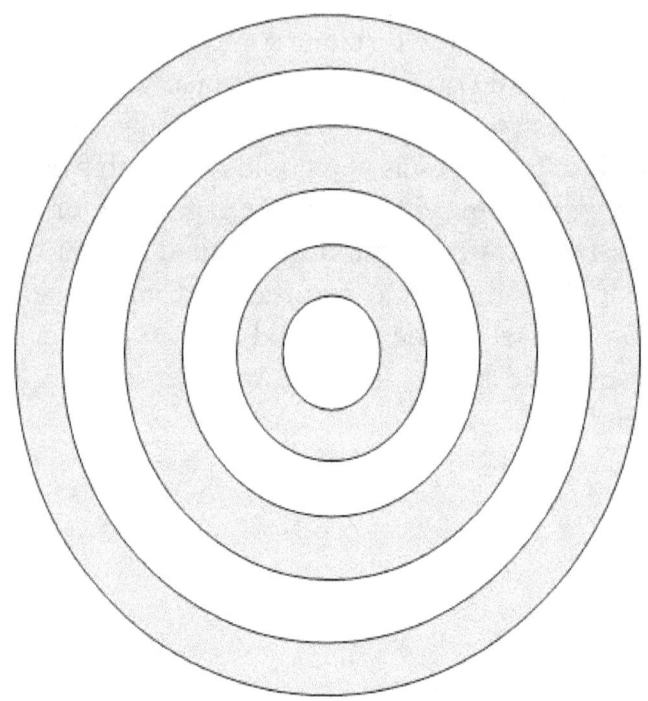

CONFLICT BULLSEYE

If you wish to write directly on the conflict target so that you can visualize things better, then by all means please do so. I want you to write the biggest conflict you have in your life, smack dab in the middle of the target--right in the bull's-eye. If it is a money matter and you're broke, write it down. If you are stuck in a bad marriage or a relationship that you know is not right for either of you, put that in the middle of the target.

You know your life better than anyone else. You must be brutally honest here, or it is all for naught. If you have been told that you are a failure and will never succeed, write it down. Place all the bad crap you have in your life all over the target. Whatever comes to your mind that represents conflict and negativity in your life, I want you to splash it all over your conflict target.

I want the biggest negative forces you have pulling at your subconscious on this target. Have you been sexually or verbally abused? Do you have family members that do not support you? Are you unhappy with your job? Are you stuck in one or many areas of your life?

Okay…now that you have this in front of you and can visually see it on paper. I want you to truly "feel" the pain associated with each of the items you wrote down. Take yourself back in time to when the event happened to you or is happening to you and really feel it! Is there a particular smell associated with any conflict or pain that you had or have in your life? Is the weather gloomy and dreary?

It should hurt. I want it to hurt, because you alone can master your mind-set to get rid of all negativity in your life; so that you can lead a more fulfilling life and get this crap behind you.

Now let's go to the Desire Bull's-eye…

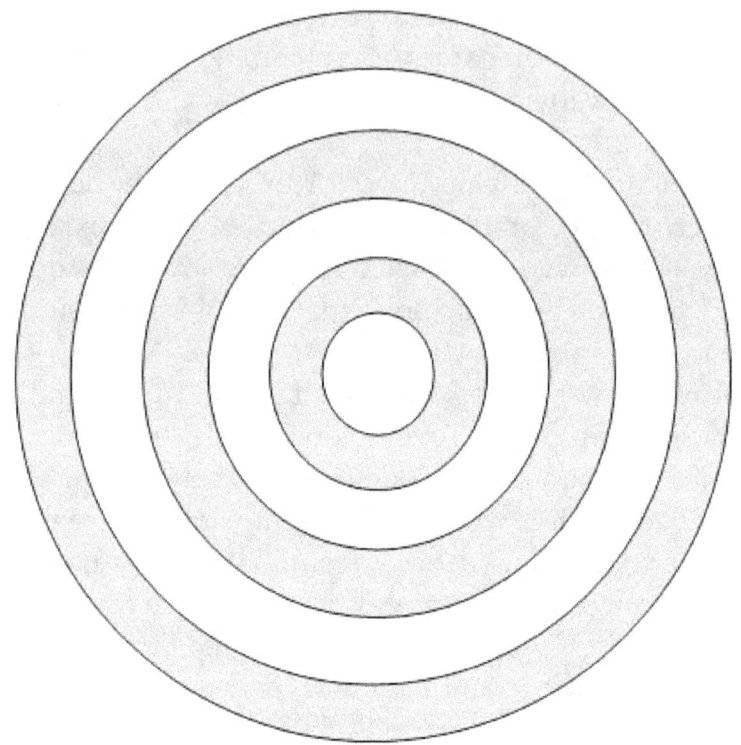

DESIRE BULLS-EYE

The Desire Bull's-eye is exactly what it is supposed to be. All the things that you desire in your life should be written down on this target. Right smack dab in the middle of the bull's-eye, write the number one thing down that you desire.

Do you desire to make more money? How about finding true love? Do you wish to have a bigger house, a fancier car, give more money to your church; or might it be something simple like having the ability to take more vacations and experiencing great memories with your loved ones? Write them all down and again, splash any and all desires you have on your desire target. Got it? Okay, great!

Now I want you to do the same thing you did with the conflict target. I want you to feel all that you desire. What does it feel like to be totally loved and adored? What does it feel like to have more money in your bank account or having a bigger house or more time to spend with your family? Get into the feeling of it. What does it smell like? Can you feel the sun's warmth on your face? Can you smell the salty sea air of being right on the beach?

What you are doing right now is rewiring your brain. Remember what I told you earlier. Your subconscious isn't that smart. It is going to believe and feel what you instruct it to do. It is really that simple. Many of you have had your desires, aspirations, and dreams crushed by others. Why? Because you allowed it to happen.

This is why I named the first part of the title of this book, "I, Alone." Only YOU can make the change, and it is up to YOU to make a decision right here and now exactly what it is you truly desire. You alone must make the decision to rid yourself of everything toxic and negative in your life. By doing so, you will feel better, you will look better, and you will attract a better energy around you for the rest of your life.

Remember what I am about to tell you right now. Your life is a story. It is your story, and your story alone! Since you are reading this book, it simply means that you have not finished writing your story. You get to write the rest of the chapters of your life any way you choose. Do you choose to live it being alive, rich, and rewarding? Or will you choose to be miserable, negative, and live in your own pity party for the rest of your life? It is your choice, and it begins and ends with you!

Now that you have your two targets, let us begin the process of crushing your conflict bull's-eye and capturing the rewards of your desires.

Since you have studied your two targets and have both of them visualized in your head, I want you to bring the image of your conflict target right in front of your face. See it as close as possible, and see and read to yourself every one of the items that you wrote down. Get those conflicts imbedded in your brain for the last time because you are about ready to obliterate them!

See this target floating right in front of you. I also want your desire target at the ready on standby, and so you can see that desire target on either side of your body. Your right side or your left side, it does not matter. Just have it at the ready.

Your conflict target is now floating right in front of you, right above your head. Now, imagine right next to you is a bow and arrow. Even if you have never shot a bow and arrow before I want you to visualize that you are an expert at it, and you can shoot a bull's-eye every single time. The conflict target is floating right in front of you, and now I want you to place it directly on the face of the sun—like you would if you were to cover the sun with this conflict target. Don't worry about staring directly at the sun for it cannot harm you. You are just visualizing and feeling everything at this point.

Take your bow and arrow and place the image of your target in front of you. Imagine that you are placing it in front of the sun. Grab your arrow and place it into the string of the bow. Now, pull it back as hard as you can with all the strength that you can muster, but do not release it just yet.

With your arm cocked back and ready to aim directly into the heart of the conflict bull's-eye, I want you to place every ounce of feeling of destroying all this negativity that has been on your shoulders for your entire life. Play some funny music in your head like circus clown music or hum to yourself the tune, "Hey, hey, hey…good-bye!"

Stare down the conflict target, funny music playing in your head, and pull back that arrow facing the sun just as hard as you can! Remember for the last time all the people that hurt you, told you that you would fail, those that abused you, called you names, bad marriages, bad business partners; and for the last time say good-bye to it all and LET THE ARROW FLY!!!

Your arrow is now piercing the heart of the conflict bull's-eye and you watch it sail right into the face of the sun! Wait for it…wait for it….do you see it now explode into the sun? Visualize it again and again in your mind so it sinks into your subconscious. You have just obliterated all negative energy and fears into the surface of the sun through your magic bow and arrow.

QUICKLY…bring your desire bull's-eye into full frame right in front of your face. All of your desires and great positive feelings and energy should be right in front of you right now! All of the negativity is gone and the only thing you should be concentrating right now is on the rich and fulfilling life you have always wanted.

This desire target is huge! It is getting bigger. As the target grows I want you to turn this target into a large beach towel, a huge beach towel that will cover your entire body. Wrap it around you right now. Everything that you wrote down on your desire target is now enveloping you and is part of your mind, body, and spirit.

Feel the love from others, feel happiness, feel the earth's and the universe's positive energy around your entire body. It feels great, doesn't it? Feel the love from your spouse or significant other; feel the power you have from having more money in your bank accounts, so you can help others and give more to your church.

Feel your business grow or a better job position opening up for you. Feel the love from your family, your children, and visualize that you are now coming from a position of strength with a newfound ability to care for your fellow man.

Instruct your subconscious that henceforth, you will no longer tolerate negativity, and you tell that brain of yours that everything and anything that you do in your life will have a positive impact on yourself and those around you. Train your brain to only look for opportunities and repel anything negative. You will not tolerate having negative conversations with your friends or family any longer.

You will be positive and upbeat, and you will SMILE more than you ever have in your entire life. Did you know that it is a proven fact that a simple smile affects others, and they see you in a different light? You will now only exude power from deep within you moving outward from your mind and body!

Watch what happens with this new power. You are like Superman, and you will not allow any kryptonite around you ever again! You can't, and you won't. It will destroy you. Keep that desire bull's-eye always at the ready if you feel you are "losing it!"

As I have mentioned to you before and I will say it again, your subconscious does not know if you are joking or being serious. You are the anti-virus software program for your brain. You now have one more tool to download into your supercomputer called your brain.

"Far better is it to dare mighty things, to win glorious triumphs, even though checkered by failure...than to rank with those poor spirits who neither enjoy nor suffer much, because they live in gray twilight that knows not victory nor defeat!"

Theodore Roosevelt

Principle #6

Love Yourself First

When I was struggling earlier in life, I never lost my sense of resolve. My parents always believed in me as they taught me to believe in myself; and they stood by my decisions, even when I made some bad ones. They let me make my own choices so I would learn from my mistakes. But I always loved myself. I admit there were times I was not happy with some of the things I did, and some of the silly decisions I made; but I never stopped loving "me" first.

So why don't people love themselves? There are many reasons for this. One of the biggest is people's failures overwhelm them. It affects their psyche, their self-worth, their self-esteem, and their general attitude towards others.

We can look at the previous chapter on negativity and how we removed it, as a basis of how your brain works against you to prevent you from loving "you" first. You have probably heard many times, "You must love yourself first before you can love others!" This is a great statement and also so very true. How the heck can you expect to give of yourself freely and love another human being, if the value you place on your self-worth is in the toilet?

People have told me, "Well, I'm not very good at that." Or they have stated to me in my workshops and seminars that their vision of themselves is not that great. How do they feel when they think about how others perceive them? Not so good, right? That kind of reflection is destructive to one's self-value. Have you ever seen someone walking down the street with their shoulders stooped over and their head hanging down looking at the ground? They are the type of person that usually claims that no one loves them, and they complain all the time why they are always broke.

Conversely, you can see someone else walking down the street, and there is a certain pep in their step. They bounce down the street with a type of swagger; their head held up high, their shoulders upright and straight, and they may even be whistling some happy tune.

These are usually your dreamers and your happy-go-lucky type of folks. They love themselves, talk richly about their friends and family, and for the most part, they love life. These are the also the same type of people that are "in love" with themselves, but that is a different chapter and book altogether.

"Okay, Ari…that is all well and good, but how do I start loving myself more?" you may ask. The answer is that it is all about attitude and perception.

Your Attitude Is Everything

I would like for you to absorb what I am about ready to tell you: God does not make junk! If you think of yourself as junk, then guess what? Your attitude will suck. If your inner attitude is poor then your outward appearance is equally as bad, is it not? Of course it is! Therefore, you can never love yourself if that is the case. Your beauty comes from the inside out.

If you were to scale your attitude from 1-10, with a 10 being the highest, where would you rank your own attitude? If you are a healthy 10, then great! If you are a 5 or below, then your inner attitude isn't so hot, is it? What do you think that does to your psyche and self-love?

All of us in this busy world are trying to accomplish so much. We have our kids in school, and we must accommodate their schedules and various sports activities.

And then we have our own problems that we deal with on a day-to-day basis, such as work and getting things accomplished at our jobs. There is a lot going on just trying to keep up, isn't there?

Sometimes, when our goals don't meet our expectations, we get into a funk. This is called disappointment. We, as humans, have a propensity to place so much pressure on ourselves that we start setting unrealistic goals and expectations. We have automatically set ourselves up for failure. The result is the lack of self-confidence.

I think everyone reading this can relate. All of this can affect your self-esteem, which I will discuss shortly; but the main thing to absorb is that your self-worth, when challenged directly or indirectly, will be affected by the attitude you have. This, in turn, will affect those around you.

Another problem with setting yourself up for disappointment is when you try to compare yourself to someone else who might be more successful than you. You might even start to compare yourself to them. That, too, can be a self-esteem and self-confidence crusher. We set lofty ambitious goals for ourselves, and when we do not reach them we may say to ourselves, "What the hell is wrong with me?" It's self-defeating. Boy, oh boy, there is a lot of "self" being thrown around here, isn't there?

A self-defeating attitude may very well affect the way you feel on a subconscious level. There I go again talking about your subconscious. Well, it's true! You can train your brain for failure, or you can look at failure, learn from it, and change your attitude and try again. And when you are done with that, you do it again.

Remember what we talked about earlier? Your subconscious does not know if you are joking with it or not. If you train your brain to be depressed, then depression is sure to follow. If you train your brain to change your attitude, how fast do you think you can change it? It can be done with the snap of a finger.

Another attitude killer is the value you place on your own self-confidence. If you have low self-confidence, it will surely affect your attitude, which affects your self-worth. Have any of you ever seen the poster of the kitten that is staring at himself in a mirror? The reflection the kitten sees of himself is that of a lion. Even though it is a little kitty cat, he perceives himself to be king of the jungle. That's attitude, self-confidence, and perception rolled into one. I love that poster.

Loving yourself first has got to start with your attitude and the way you perceive yourself—not the way others perceive you. If you do not exude your inner beauty, which is one of your greatest assets, then how the heck can others truly love you for who you are?

Loving yourself first also comes from the perception you have of yourself. Let me ask you this question: Do you embrace the positive qualities you have? Let's discuss this for minute. You have been blessed with so many awesome attributes, and some of you do not even realize it. Those attributes are a gift, and so many people squander that gift.

How about certain skills you may have that others do not have? Do you speak another language? What about certain talents or athletic abilities you may have that others do not possess?

When I was younger, I was on the tennis team in high school. I was pretty good at it, but I knew that I would never play in the finals at Wimbledon. It was not because I didn't have the desire. I have plenty of that. But to get to a level of greatness on a championship level is a gift that I simply did not have.

I also play a great round of golf. I had delusions of being on the PGA Tour. But that wasn't going to happen because God did not bless with me that particular type of talent. It is a gift to play like a Jack Nicklaus, a Phil Mickelson, or a Tiger Woods. They also had the tenacity to go out and hit a million golf balls on the driving range every single day of their lives. But it still requires a gift.

I love the game of golf. I love the comradery, the sport, the rules of the game; and I love the mental aspect you absolutely must have. You must have that element to play a sport where you chase a ball around a very large piece of real estate. Does it affect my attitude? Absolutely not! I know my limitations. Now I just enjoy the game.

I have never met a championship athlete of any kind that hated himself. I know athletes I have worked with that did not have their heads screwed on straight, but it does not mean that they did not love themselves. From my earlier comment, you could probably have a chuckle that most professional athletes are "in love" with themselves. That is probably not too far from the truth.

An interesting point I would like to make here is that if you have a low self-esteem, if you do not love yourself or lack complete confidence in your own abilities, people will pick up on that. Those around you are not stupid. They will zero in on your lack of "self," and since you are not stupid either, you are going to sense that feedback from them.

This can directly affect the perception of what you think of yourself. You may see the lion in the mirror, but the feeling of lack of self-worth may reduce and tame you to become a pussy cat very quickly. Attitude, baby, attitude!

As you are already aware, your supercomputer brain is highly complex. It can take you from a state of euphoria, and all of a sudden you can get a phone call and that call or conversation can bring you down like a ton of bricks. The interesting thing that happens to you at this point is how you handle that swing of emotions.

Why do some people handle it better than others? It's because their subconscious has been programmed differently to handle that type of stress or emotional swing. I cannot stress to you, my dear readers, how this plays on your psyche and your ability, or lack thereof, to deal with situations that change and alter the perception you have of yourself.

Ultimately, this can screw with your self-esteem. Low self-esteem, low self-worth, and low self-confidence will indeed draw that kind of negative influence in your life. You can and will draw-in unhappy relationships or bad business dealings, and it may very well prevent you from receiving a pay increase or job promotion.

What does this do? It screws with your mind, makes you unhappy, or worse—depressed; and you might then feel the entire world is against you. Your sense of value at this point might very well be thrown out the window. How do you love yourself now? Not very well, right?

Do you recall what I said starting out in this chapter? I told you that my parents taught me to always believe in myself. This is a huge nugget I want you to take away about loving yourself first. Your belief system and your mind-set must be so stinking strong that the way in which you believe in yourself will help you love yourself first.

You have to believe in YOU! You must believe in your God-given abilities and have confidence in those abilities, which will make you stronger as you progress through life…no matter how old you are. It is never too late to adopt these principals.

Your Brain Needs Goals To Love

Your belief system is one thing, but there is also another force at play here. Of the people I have met all over the world, one of the most interesting things I have found is you can separate the people that don't love themselves from the people that do rather easily.

There is actually a common denominator, and I bet you will never guess what it is. The people that have low self-esteem, low self-confidence, and low self-worth are typically the people that have no goals in life. Isn't that interesting? I'm not talking about setting a goal. I'm talking about people not having any goals or ambitions whatsoever.

The funny thing about that is that we know people like this. Think about it for a minute. If one does not think highly of one self, what are the chances of them being successful in their life? More importantly, what are their goals?

A person that tells me they have no goals is a person that has already determined their own fate. Without goals, the road you travel will be on a one-way dead end street. Let me repeat this so it is clear. Without goals, you are not going very far. You won't travel, you won't see the world, and you will never get to help other people.

Without goals, you will eventually end up hating yourself for not having any. People without goals are terrified of any positive outcome so they either quit, or they never get started in the first place.

What do you think that does to someone's belief system? What do you think it does to their psyche? What do you think it does to the value they place on themselves? And finally, the last question is: How much do you think they love themselves?

The answers are self-evident as I have savvy readers. But seriously folks…if you wish to implement an idea and are ambitious enough to go for it, then you must first believe in yourself. More importantly you must love yourself for who you are and be aware of the abilities that each of us was born with. Without those two ingredients, you might very well stay in, draw the blinds, and call it a day.

A goal might very well set your mind at ease. Look at it this way. If you do nothing but then you find yourself doing something that makes you happy, you just might want more of it because it makes you happy.

If something makes you happy, might you be more inclined or less inclined to do it again? If you do it again, then guess what you just did? You just set a goal. A small one at that, but you set a goal nonetheless. If that goal turns into a hobby or better yet, a passion, then you are on your way to changing your belief system, your mind-set, and whole bunch other things that will trigger happiness.

If a goal gives you aspirations and gets you motivated, would it not also make you happy? For you to be happy, you truly must love yourself. Why do you think that is?

Remember what I stated earlier? Beauty comes from within! How can a flower blossom without the earth providing the nutrients, the love of nature and the warmth of the sun?

In other words, your inner beauty is a direct reflection of you! If you do not connect with your inner beauty, you make it hard to love yourself. It will be very difficult for you to blossom, you will not feel the warmth of another human being; and you will never receive the nourishment of love.

So a goal, any goal that will get you to be positive, and gets you to think on an unselfish basis, is a goal worth striving for. You got my vote on that one.

Self Love and Relationships

Loving yourself first may sometimes be a little confusing to a few of you. Allow me to explain. Some people think it a fable that in order to lead a happy and stable life you must love yourself first. That may be well and true, but it is not necessary always the case.

One may suffer from being too self-absorbed, or perhaps you have heard it as being self-centered or having too much self-interest. This is more ego driven and more self-serving than it is of loving one's self.

The problem here isn't that man thinks too highly of himself—the problem is that man thinks too low of himself. People can sometimes be victims of their own circumstances as they go through life with low self-esteem, low personal and/or self-worth, and of course, no sense of feeling significant.

The latter is by far the most damaging because all of us wish to feel that we are important. We place tremendous value on what others think about us, and we as a people need that sense of significance to help feel loved.

We do this in relationships as well. Sometimes we do not get what we truly want out of a relationship, and it diminishes our sense of significance. Some of the great scholars talk about how we must have significance in a relationship, and they are right.

But what if you are in a relationship and the other person tells you that they do not love you anymore? Or they may say to you, "You don't do it for me anymore." Maybe they are not getting from you what they need in a relationship, and the only way they know how to get out of the relationship is to attack you. This way they can feel more significant about themselves.

It is not the fact that self-love is missing here. Love is the element that is missing. Your partner telling you that they do not love you anymore is them really saying to you, "I love myself more than I do you, and you don't do it for me anymore!" Don't take it personally. It's not you.

That is just their way of dealing with their own lack of self-love and protecting themselves for not having it in the first place. It is easier to attack someone than to admit it and say, "I'm very sorry that I am leaving you, but I don't love myself. If I stay in this relationship with you, I may hurt you emotionally, and I love you too much to do that to you." That's not something you hear every day, is it? And you probably won't either.

Trust me, you are better off without that person in your life as that is shallow, hurtful, and never a good recipe for a loving, lasting relationship. In my last book, "The Reference Point," I was very clear on relationships and what to look for and what not to look for in a relationship. It is germane to our topic here so it deserves mentioning again.

If you are single, do yourself a favor. When you meet someone that you have taken a liking to, just ask them one simple question. Ask the other person to describe to you their last relationship. If they speak ill of the other person and trash talk them, then you know this is a person you must avoid.

Leave skid marks behind you if you have to because there is damage, and you are going to receive the exact same treatment. I promise you. Someone that behaves in this manner typically has low self-esteem, and as I stated above, it is easier to attack someone else than admit the fact that they are the person that is damaged. Remember about significance?

People need to feel a sense of worth and a sense power over other human beings. Not because the other person may be weaker, but because they need to make themselves feel better about themselves because of the self-love they do not possess.

Use that as your reference point, and you will easily detect if a person loves themselves or even likes themselves, for that matter. You may argue that a person can love themselves and still verbally or physically attack another person. And that would be a valid point. But if you can sort out those that love themselves and don't attack, as opposed to the ones that love themselves and do attack, with whom would you rather spend quality time? Good! I'm glad you agree.

Love has no selfishness. Love has no jealousy, and love is not evil. Love is also very persistent, isn't it? We do strange things for love, don't we? I know everyone reading this can relate to that. Actually, I think everyone on the planet can relate that love will make you do some crazy stuff, right?

A person who truly loves another human being will be tender, patient, and will extend tremendous kindness and humanity. Love is sincere, it is warm, and it is living life fully and unconditionally. Love has no borders, it should not have any conditions, and it has tremendous tolerance. None of these are at your disposal if you do not love yourself first. It is an impossibility.

> *"Perhaps we shall learn, as we pass through this age, that the 'other self' is more powerful than the physical self we see when we look into the mirror."*
>
> *Napoleon Hill*

Principle #7

Serve Others

The cool part about this last principle is that serving others has *everything* to do with the other six principles. Let me explain and come clean with you, my dear readers.

You are never going to fully master all of the seven principles. I know, I know—how dare I say that, right? If you are consistent with the principles I have presented, you will, with time, get good at them. Perhaps you will even become great at them, but you will never "master" them.

To master anything, you must always be the student. "But Ari, I am not in school anymore," you may state. Let me share with you the following: the greatest teachers in the world are always studying to become better at their craft.

I didn't call this book, "Try to Master" or "See if you can Master." I called it, "I, Alone! Mastering Life's Seven Principles." The key words in this title are "I, Alone." It must start with you because *you* are the only one that can make the decision to take the first step to become better at anything. Whatever it is you wish to attempt, you and you alone, must make the decision to put the first foot forward.

I didn't title this book to torment you in any way with my last statement. I did it to give you a heads-up that in order to master these seven principles, you must be awesome at the first six first. Here's the deal. I designed it that way. You cannot be effective and great with Principle #7 until you understand and are great at the first six. Again, let me explain.

In order to be effective at serving others and to do it with passion and unconditionally, you must make great decisions. In order to understand how to serve others, you must strive to be better tomorrow than you were today.

You must carry yourself with dignity and be of the highest integrity if you are to serve others properly. In order to "teach" others to serve others, you must have wisdom. Serving others unselfishly and with no personal agenda requires that you eliminate everything negative in your life. And last, but not least, in order to serve others, you must love yourself first so others will feel that the sincerity is truly from your heart.

These are the principles. I live my life, and it took me a very long to get it right. And I can tell you honestly that I, too, have not mastered them; but I am great at them, and I strive for excellence so that I stay true to these principles for the rest of my life.

It is a commitment that I made to myself over 20 years ago, but didn't write these down because I didn't come up with them back then. It took years and years of self-development and studying human behavior to figure it out.

The one thing I have discovered about people, whether they live in this part of the world or on the other side of the planet, is people form certain habits—good and bad. From those habits you can determine the way people think, walk, talk, and socially interact.

Let's start off by discussing ways in which we should serve others.

Serving Unselfishly

Serving unselfishly is by far one of the most important things that should be a priority when you serve others. I will not dwell on it too long, but long enough to have you absorb my foundation of thought.

I have often seen people, celebrities, and sports figures give to various charities and foundations. Good for them! For the most part, their heart is in the right place, and they do a good job of spreading their wealth to those in need and who are suffering throughout the world.

However, many do it for the attention and the "look what I did this week," type of fame. This is not serving unselfishly. If you are in a position to give to others and you serve with your heart, you cannot be in it for self-glory or to deliberately bring attention to yourself. That defeats the purpose of giving unselfishly.

To serve unselfishly means you either don't want the attention or you don't need it. The glory of serving and the wonderful feeling you get by serving, without seeking attention, is precisely the point.

I remember many years ago when I was in Mexico. One of my favorite places to go is either Cozumel or Puerto Vallarta or "PV" as we affectionately call it. PV used to be a quaint little fishing village built next to the jungle with cobblestone streets. Today it is a bustling city full of life, and buildings and hotels are going up everywhere you turn. Right in the middle of town there is a beautiful old church named, "Our Lady of Guadalupe."

Late one afternoon I was walking through town, going in and out of the many thousands of storefronts doing a little shopping. Next to the church you can see many vendors selling their wares as well as the little food trucks selling "real" street tacos. Even though many may warn you not to eat from the street trucks in Mexico, I think they are just as good as some of the restaurants; and you ain't living unless you have a street taco right off the cart in a little town in Mexico.

As I passed by the church there was an older lady, just as sweet as she could be, sitting on a tattered blanket right next to the curb of the church. A little girl about 10 years of age, perhaps the lady's granddaughter, offered to sell me some Chicklets gum. Those of you who have been to this part of the world know that the children will often run up to you on the beach or on the street to sell you Chicklets gum.

I said in my best guttural Spanish, "No, gracias," and I walked past the both of them. After a few steps, I stopped, turned around and went back to the lady and the little girl. A few feet away from them I saw a man standing near the church, and waved to him to come over to me. I asked him if he spoke English and he nodded.

"Can you ask this lady and the little girl in Spanish, what happened to them to place them on the streets to beg?" He looked at me and said, "This is a very poor country, senor. Many turn to Christ and ask Him to send us good people that will give freely of their hearts to help us in our time of need." I took in what he told me and said to him, "Just ask her that question please? I want to know why she is here today."

He nodded and then conveyed my question to her in Spanish. She looked at me and then turned to the man. She then answered my question. When she stopped talking, he looked at me and translated. He told me that her life was one of shattered dreams. Her husband and her son were fishermen, and both of their lives were taken by the sea. Her family's dream was to have a little fish shop to cater to the tourists and to supply fresh fish to the locals.

After their death, she was left to take care of her granddaughter and was left penniless as her only skill was that of a cook and sewing clothes. She could not read nor write her own name.

I think many of you know where I am going with this story. Yes, I gave her money and many of you would argue with me that you should never give money to those who beg as they will either buy drugs or booze. Since I do not believe for a minute that it was a staged con, her story impacted me and I will remember this event for the rest of my life. This event happened over 20 years ago.

I reached into my wallet and pulled out a crisp $100 bill and handed it to her. She looked at me like I had just given her the winning lottery ticket. Our translator friend did the sign of the cross. "Thank you senor for being so kind to her. She is such a beautiful person, and she deserves it and needs that money so much."

The woman started to cry and her granddaughter started hugging me, "Gracias, senor, gracias. Muchas gracias!" The lady turned to our translator and started speaking to him again in Spanish. He told me, "She told me to tell you that God is going to bless you greatly for what you have done for me today." Tears started swelling in my eyes. I just looked at her and to her, "De nada. De nada." (No worries.)

It filled my heart with great joy to be able to do this for this lovely lady and her granddaughter. That money probably fed her for a month. I did not need the glory, I asked for nothing in return, and I put a smile on three peoples' lives. And, by the way, our translator asked nothing for himself even though I offered him what little I had left in my wallet. He would not take it. He just wanted me to give to the woman and the little girl.

Let's get back to those of you that would never give any money to a panhandler, as you may call them. You give what you can, and if you choose not to give then that is your choice. You don't want to contribute to someone's drug habit or drinking problem, and I get that.

I have news for you—some of the people you see under a bridge or by the side of the road did not choose this lifestyle. Instead of saying to yourself *they are drunks or drug addicts*, be positive and think that you just offered them hope.

But what exactly are you giving them? That is not the question you should be asking yourself. The question is what did you just do to change someone else's life and do it without conditions? Did you have to cash-in your 401K or refinance your house to offer kindness to a stranger? You are giving them a pittance. What is more important to learn here is the reward you receive. You are getting favor from God and placed a smile on another human being's face. What is that worth?

What is the feeling you have inside when you give freely of yourself and ask nor expect anything in return? When you do it unselfishly, the feeling in your heart is euphoric. You cannot describe it because it cannot be measured or placed into words. If you have felt this before, then you know exactly what I am talking about.

If you have never experienced the feeling you get in your gut and your heart, then that is a signal that you are not serving unselfishly. You are expecting either something in return or an acknowledgment for your actions.

The Note From Above

I speak of God because I am a Christian, but I do not wish to speak of Our Heavenly Father to those that may have another power that you praise or worship. Those are your choices of faith, and I respect that of you. Please respect that for me—as I believe all things go through Christ. That is my belief, and that faith has gotten me through some very dark times.

With that being said, I want to teach you about "The Note From Above." It is a "feel good" ideal and even simpler to implement. It should have a huge and significant impact on your life, but more importantly it should have a much greater impact on those that you may or may not even know.

We have all had our share of struggles in life. Goodness gracious, I have certainly had my share of them, that's for sure. We all know a family that is in need, a church that requires money for whatever reason, or a family that may have lost a son or daughter in the war. Perhaps you know of a school that is in dire need of books, supplies, or computers.

Sometimes on television you may see a family that has been wiped out by an act of force majeure like a tornado, a flood, or even a forest fire. I've often tried to place myself in their shoes to understand what it may feel like to lose everything in a disaster. It is very hard thing to do, and if you have never experienced that, one can only imagine. They may have been the lucky ones to have escaped with their lives, but all their mementos, their family photos, treasures, and their homes—all gone in the blink of an eye.

Maybe you have seen other television commercials that inform you "for pennies a day" you can sponsor an orphan or rescue an animal from being put down. We've all seen spots on TV such as this. The question I have for you is this: How many of you have actually followed through with any of these categories and have given whatever you can to help out?

The answer would shock you as I know for a fact how few the numbers are of people that will actually step up to serve others in need. People acknowledge that they have seen these "call to action" campaigns. The sad thing is that very few of us have followed through with serving. It is unfortunate that sometimes tragedy must hit close to home before we, as a people, take action. The great part about it is when we do step up, we are great at it!

So I put forth a challenge to you that I call "The Note From Above" because it is exactly what it should be. It's a note out of thin air, a note from heaven, a note that changes the course of the way we in which look at humanity.

Remember what I said about "I, Alone?" It is *you* that must take the first step. In order to take a first step, you must change something in your day-to-day routine that places you on a new path. Even if you do it to change one of the seven principles, you have at least done something to alter your course. When you do this you will change peoples' lives, including your own.

Go to a local card store, and buy a ton of blank greeting cards without a message so you may tailor it with your own words. When you purchase them, I request that you are very keen in your thought and intentions as to what you will be doing with these cards.

Do you realize the impact you will have to send a card to one of your friends that is struggling? "Just thinking of you in your time of need and letting you know that angels are always around you," is one message that you may write down. No signature, no return address--just a note from above that let's someone know that are in your thoughts and prayers.

Maybe you place a $20 bill or a gift card from your local grocer. "The Note From Above" has special significance to send to a disaster victim. They don't know you anyway, so placing your return address on it means that you are waiting for acknowledgment for your good deed. This is not doing something unselfish or having your own agenda in mind.

Serve another family by dropping food off on their doorstep with the anonymous "Note From Above" simply saying, "Angels are with you to bless you and your family!" It matters not if you believe in angels. Perhaps the family that you help does.

When you see a family on TV that has lost everything in an act of force majeure, call up the news desk of the station and ask how you may get in touch with that family to send them a card or money. If you cannot afford to send them anything but a card, then just send that card by itself. That touch—that reaching out to another human being is so rewarding you cannot even imagine what it will do to that family.

Do you have the ability to drop off a laptop computer to school that is in dire need of one or two? Ship it UPS with a blank "Note From Above," and say, "I hope this small token goes a long way to help your students." This changes lives my dear readers.

Write "The Note From Above" to an orphanage and include a gift card for ice cream for the kids. The card says, "Have a cool day kids and smile—someone loves you!"

Your church or any house of worship is always in need of something. Maybe they need money for a retreat for kids, a group of battered women or children from abused families. Or how about sending "The Note From Above" to a woman's shelter along with a jumbo-sized package of diapers?

There are so many things you can do to touch another human being's life. Sending your clothes to Goodwill is most honorable; but once it goes into the chute, you have no idea where it goes, do you? "The Note From Above" gives it the close and personal touch so that you know where it is going, and you know exactly what family or child you are affecting.

Your brain needs that close association to have the good chemicals come out and give you that sense of euphoria. When you give freely of yourself, it tickles the pleasure sensors, and we are most certainly not tickling our pleasure sensors enough, are we? Be careful how you answer that question!

"The Note From Above," only works if you give from your heart, and you do it unselfishly. Many of you are so very generous, and I thank you for the bottom of my heart for those lives that you touch. Keep it up!

Serving Your Mind

Throughout our journey together we have discussed, and hopefully discovered, so many ways your brain and more specifically, your subconscious, works against you. What if you could serve your brain? What do I mean by that? It starts by you putting yourself into a place where only great thought, spirit, and love come together in a cohesive bond to give you tremendous power with others.

Keep in mind I didn't say power "over" others. I said power "with" others. Remember about negativity? Well, what if you could put yourself into place where you just dreamed and served your brain with nothing but great food. You served it nothing but positive stuff.

There is a spiritual connection we have with all things—especially people; and even though your heart needs to be in the right place to serve others, if your brain is not engaged in super brain activity, then you are only working with half your power.

Imagine your brain being completely empty. You now get to start all over right now. Begin by removing all that is bad, and get rid of all the junk that you think is inside your brain that should not be there in the first place. Go ahead, try it. Lie on the floor or sit in your favorite chair. Get comfortable.

Close your eyes and put yourself into a little meditative state of mind. Remember how we looked at the desire target a while back? Do the same thing here. Clear your mind and remove everything in your brain. All of it! Get rid of all the crap in your head. Bad relationships, abuse, alcoholism, poor decision making, drug abuse, bad thoughts, dead end job, past marital problems…all gone. Everything in your past is now history, and the great thing about history is that it is behind all of us.

There is nothing in your brain but space. The great thing is that right now you get fill your brain with whatever cool stuff you want to place inside. I call this "The Dream Maker." Anything and everything you do henceforth is new to your brain. You get to create all that is good, and get to fill it with whatever greatness, wonder and imagination you want.

So now what? What do you want to fill it with? It's your brain, so start filling it? But wait! The first thing you fill it with could be the most important item, so what is it going to be? It's a little tough isn't it? What would you place in first? You are serving your brain great food for thought right now and it's your choice, but let me give you a little help and then you can choose on your own, okay?

How about we start off with the obvious—love and the warmth of loving everyone around you. Love is everything as we are all aware, but I want you to do something extraordinary right now. I want you to write a mental love letter to your brain every day for the rest of your life. That's right! Start programming your brain and tell yourself how much you love yourself every single day. Write that note to your brain and say it in the mirror every day you wake up.

I could have used this in the last chapter, but I chose to save it for here, because now you know nothing of hate, prejudice or hurt. All you know is that you love your fellow man as equally as you love your enemy. Henceforth, you no longer have enemies. You love everyone equally.

Next, let's put in a heaping spoonful of tolerance. You see yourself being more tolerant with your children, perhaps an elderly parent you are taking care of or possessing more tolerance with your spouse. You see yourself being more tolerant with the people you work with. If you are the boss, your employees are everything to you, and you are tolerant of their mistakes; and you make sure they understand that you care about their success.

Now let's throw in a big scoop of forgiveness. This will be tough for some of you because many have been screwed over in business, or maybe a spouse, partner, or significant other cheated on you. Maybe you have lost someone close to you that was killed by a drunk driver, was raped, or perhaps brutally murdered. This is your chance to start over with your mind.

Sometimes the act of forgiveness is one of the greatest yet toughest acts to show others. But it is essential if you are to serve others. You cannot teach what you do not know…or feel. When you forgive, it not only removes a burden that may otherwise be with you for the rest of your life, but your brain appreciates the fact that you give it a rest sometimes.

Having hate in your heart makes your brain work overtime, and more brain space is required for hate than for love. You're doing great! I'm very proud of you. Let's keep going.

Hmmm….let's see what is missing here. We've got love loaded in first, along with loving your fellow man. Then we put in heaping spoonful of tolerance and then a big scoop of forgiveness. We still have plenty of room, so what would you place in next? How about music? How did I come up with music? Because music is the heartbeat of life, and the first beat we hear is that of our mother's heart while still in the womb.

Your own music is your lifeblood, and it is also the rhythm of the world and the universe. Music is in our soul; it is our passion and is a huge part of the foundation of our memories. You remember so much from music: a first kiss or the time when you were young in school. That tune can come on the radio, and it transports you back immediately to a place and time in your past. But let's put in great music. If you are not a lover of classical music like Beethoven, Mozart, or Chopin, then put some in your brain.

Classical music is the basis of all other music, and if you fill your brain with garbage music, then you are defeating the purpose of this exercise. But alas, it is your mind, and you are free to do as you choose.

The next thing I want you to place in your brain is knowledge! But it's got to be good knowledge. Your brain is a supercomputer, and I want you to place in great, powerful knowledge that will make your brain strong and give you more food for thought, i.e. books about the arts, history, language, science, and poetry.

Give yourself the gift of knowledge, and you will become a great teacher and a wonderful servant of mankind. Knowledge will give you the strength of the earth's strongest tree, and you will be deeply rooted and connected to all living things.

Next, we want to place in our brains something very special. How about some new memories? Here is "The Dream Mind." You get to create any new memory you want. Was there something that you wanted to do all your life and never had a chance to do? Go ahead and place that inside your brain now. Is there someone in your life that you never told how you felt about them? Put that image of telling them that in your brain. How about a place you have always wanted to go? Put that in your dream brain and feel the beach, the sand, the warm water, or the history of that city. Is love missing in your life? Place that dream person in your brain right now, and he or she shall come to you. Whatever it is that you wish to serve your brain, do so now.

If you have done this little Dream Mind exercise, you should be feeling a lot of emotions right now. You cannot serve others well if your brain is not receptive and filled with the basic ingredients we just placed inside. Your service to mankind will be significant, your service to community will be wonderfully fulfilling, and your service to others will indeed be rewarded. It will come back to you tenfold. You must have faith in yourself first, and trust your heart. The rest you can make up as you go along. Serving your brain good food will help you nourish others forever.

It's The Small Things That Count

I bet everyone can go back in time and remember when your parents made you do chores. It was terrible. We used to visit our relatives in good ole Pine Bluff, Arkansas. We lovingly called ourselves the Arkansas Greek hillbillies. My cousin Tommy and I thought we were being punished by being sent out to my aunt and uncle's very large yard to go pull weeds. It was torture—living hell.

During the summer kids want to go to the pool, have fun, and be kids. But no! We were sent to the yard to go pull weeds. It was one of those hot Arkansas summers that was sticky humid, which would drain you of strength. Anyone that lives in a very humid part of our country knows exactly what I am talking about. There was nothing you wanted more than to be inside where the house was cool, and the air was blowing on your face from the breeze of the ceiling fan. That was living life! Not pulling stinking weeds.

My other cousin Katie, Tommy's sister, was not going to pull weeds. She was too sophisticated to pull weeds, plus she's a girl. We had no chance of sucking her into those chores. So Katie would run by us guys and just snicker, give us a tsk tsk, and she'd then drive off with her friends to the country club. There she would get to go swimming and play tennis. Damn the luck!

So Tommy and I would be out there for hours upon hours. We used our imagination to concoct any excuse we could think of to release ourselves out of weed bondage. We were so desperate to get out of "weed pulling hell" that one day we actually performed an Indian rain dance right on the driveway of the house with the hope of it pouring. Of course, it never did.

I would get the lid to the trash can and find a stick, and I would beat it like a drum to get any kind of reaction out of the rain gods! "Ohhh yaaa yaa ohh ya yaa hmmmm oy yaa yaa," we would chant in our best tribal voices. Nothing! I think the best we could muster was to bring a cloud into frame on an otherwise cloudless day. We thought we were onto something. But alas…nothing! I remember those days as if they were yesterday. Sure, we had our fun at the pool, but I want to make a point here.

The moral of this story is that if you are to serve and serve with honor, dignity, and be unselfish, there will be times when you have to pull weeds. Pulling weeds makes your house beautiful. Your house, in this case, is your spiritual house. When you pull weeds, you get to clear clutter, and when the clutter is gone, you have something new and fresh in its place. You can then plant flowers and be in harmony with the earth you help groom.

Serving your community will require you to pull weeds and get your hands dirty. When you serve to put a fresh coat of paint on your church, build new stands at your high school stadium, or gather trash at the YMCA, you will have to pull weeds. So what if you get dirt under your fingernails. You did something great, even if it is a small gesture. It is the little things that count. Those little things—those little chores will make you great.

Have any of you mentored a young boy or girl? Perhaps you have had your kids go to work with you. Maybe you are part of Big Brothers or Big Sisters? If you are, then you are helping change a child's life that otherwise might not have had the opportunity to learn from you.

Mentoring gives you the chance to change the direction of a youth's life to stay away from drugs or to keep him or her away from a gang. To serve in this fashion, you must pull weeds. You are helping them get rid of all the bad stuff surrounding their life, and you get to tend to their garden to give them your positive insight on life. You help plant better ideals to strengthen their belief system. It's the small things you do that makes for great change.

What about serving the elderly? It reminds me of Joe and Sarah earlier in the book. They have long since passed I am afraid, but who took care of them in their final days? During my mother Penelope's last days, I moved into the house to take care of her.

I gave her the best attention I could and made her breakfast, lunch, and dinner. She also had a huge sweet tooth, and I had to monitor her sugar intake, but who was I kidding. If she wanted some ice cream, I gave her ice cream. Why would I deny an old woman some mint chocolate chip? It's my mother and she deserved every scoop!

I went through cancer treatment with her, which she eventually beat, and about eight months before her death she had to have a bowel resection. I sat in the hospital with her and made sure she ate her dinner, per her doctor's orders. Of course, she wanted pie and ice cream. Go figure!

For my mother, it was the small things that put a smile on her face. I could bring her a sandwich I just made in her kitchen, and she would look at me with her loving eyes and say, "Oh, Ari...how wonderful. I bet it is the best sandwich ever. Do I get ice cream after this?" Of course I would just chuckle.

There is no greater feeling in the world than to serve the elderly for they have served their entire lives, and it is time to give back to them in their final days before meeting their maker.

Let be very clear on something here. If you have ever had a falling out with your parents, please do yourself a favor and make peace with them before they pass. These small things make you great, and to serve in this fashion will not only make you feel better, but it will give you peace of mind.

Don't let the small things get in your way of being great because you may regret it for the rest of your life. Remember the expression, "Don't sweat the small stuff?" Well then, don't. It will eat at you, and life is way too short to sweat the small stuff, right? Spending time with the elderly are the times that you listen and you learn. You never know what small nuggets of wisdom you may pick up. These are good words to remember and great brain food for your soul.

Serving The Sick and Special Needs

I truly believe God has a plan for us when a child is stricken with a terminal illness and loses their battle to various forms of disease. It breaks my heart to see a child suffer, and my prayers go out to the parents. But there is a divine plan for us and a lesson to be learned from it.

It is all about love. It is the love we have for a sick child, and the love that child brings to all people around them. These children are truly a gift, and they are very, very special. There are so many stories about children that stare death right in the face yet their attitude is positive; they are stronger than most adults and many have no fear of dying. They are incredible and they should inspire us all.

The amazing and miraculous part of death is that it brings forth life! Foundations get established, and people are more inclined to donate money to help fund the development for a potential cure. In no other time in history have we seen hospitals build additions to their buildings to house new technology. These techno wonders are increasing our lifespan, and we now have new ways to discover illnesses far quicker than we ever have before. The advancement in this science is mind-boggling. It is saving lives!

There are many who do not wish to serve the sick, and that is your choice. Many fear hospitals and I even have friends that won't go near them because of that reason. But you deny yourself the service of love for if it is you that brings a smile to a sick child's face. How can you experience that kind of fulfillment if you have never done it before?

Go serve on a fundraiser for a child. Go see that child and read him or her a story. Go help a hospital with their programs for children that are recovering from cancer. You will be lucky to have done so and it will change your life, I promise you.

I am also completely impressed, and in total awe with nurses, social workers and the staff that attend to our special needs children. I love all nurses, and we should all be thankful for what they do. They are amazing individuals, but I will say this to you; it requires a very special person with the patience of Job to work with special needs children. God bless you all, and I wish there were many more of you out there in the world. I truly believe in my heart that these people are really angels sent from heaven above.

Let me tell you a story about one such angel. It is my older brother, Bill Priakos. Brother Bill has three fabulous boys: Bill Jr., Jason, and Christian. I say "boys" lovingly as all of my nephews are fine young adults now, and we are all extremely proud of them all. Christian is a special needs young man as he was born with Downs Syndrome. He is a remarkable individual and possesses a wonderfully wicked and keen sense of humor. The kid is full of love, a big hugger, and he just loves to laugh and have fun.

However, many years ago while Christian was still a young boy, Bill was on the Development Disability Board in Arkansas. You see, back in the 1950s older buildings were converted to help serve children with various degrees of disability, and some of these disabilities were quite severe.

So for years, Bill had an unwavering passion to help de-institutionalize the "system" and push forth an agenda to give special needs children a chance to optimize their lives. With so many legal hurdles and obstacles to overcome, many people would have given up at this stage of the game, but quitting is just not in the Priakos' blood--so Bill forged on.

My brother is very humble and while writing this part of the book he told me, "Ari...at least I got a chance to serve, in a very small way, but serve nonetheless." But the change he had to first overcome was to change the mind-set about the way people thought of the handicapped, as they were termed back then.

The changes Bill helped to implement were monumental, and they were accomplished by a ton of hard work, a never quit attitude, and a few miracles along the way. Because of his tenacity, and in no "small way," so many families with special needs children now benefit from new types treatment, a better quality of care and, of course, more angels to look after them.

If you have never been around a child with special needs or do not know of a family that has a child like this, you cannot comprehend the years and years that it took to get government on the same page to ensure a better quality of life for these children.

So to my brother Bill…thank you for your tireless effort to help out not only your son, but so many, many families as well. They do indeed benefit from your years of hard work with all the love you put into it, and deep from your heart. Bless you. Now as an adult, Christian is a man of responsibility. He lives in his own apartment, has a job, takes care of his chores, and is a great member of society.

Just to let you what a character my nephew is, one time at Christmas we were at Bill's oldest son's house, Bill Jr. Either Jason or Bill Jr. gave Christian a Mr. Mike as a present. This was a state-of-the-art contraption, had all the attachments with all the bells and whistles, and came with its own way to store a plethora of music.

Well, let me tell you, we created a monster. Christian flipped over this thing. He's a pretty quick study and had the dang thing figured out in no time at all. Well, that is where he came unglued. He excused himself to one of the upstairs bedrooms, and we literally did not see him for two days.

I think he thought he was Kenny Rogers or some famous singer because he wore that machine out. He was so engrossed in that machine that we had to bring food up to him so he would eat. I'm telling you, the kid had smoke coming out of his ears…and the machine, too! Ah…what a great memory!

So when I say to you that God has a plan for us when someone is stricken with an illness, I mean that it is a time for reflection, a time for being blessed, and a time to give thanks. Not just to be thankful that you have the gift of health, but also your ability to serve others who are less fortunate than you.

Those whose days are numbered are touched with your grace, your smile, and your attention. You cannot replace that feeling of joy when you give so lovingly to another human being. If you serve in this capacity you will be blessed with peace, and you will always walk righteously.

Before I end this book I want to leave you with a few last thoughts. IT IS NOT ABOUT YOU! It is never about you, and it can never be about you. It is about serving others, and by helping others get what they want, you shall receive what you want by default. It is just the way the universe is balanced.

Serving others must be pure, and you must give of yourself with every fiber of your being. Do so with love in your heart, with deep feeling and with compassion for your fellow man. Go forth and serve with honor as it will make you whole with yourself, and you will be blessed with a good name.

Go forth and serve others with your knowledge and your wisdom for you will help others to think for themselves. Go forth and serve others to be better in their lives, their marriages, and their businesses, for you are a steward of education. Go forth and help people be more positive, and help them to keep evil out of their lives.

Go forth and help people understand to love themselves first for that gift is contagious. Go forth and help others, and serve to the best of your ability. Doing so will give you happiness, and it will keep you young and alive.

"One can have no smaller or greater mastery than mastery of oneself!"

Leonardo da Vinci

Conclusion and Acknowledgement

I dedicated the last book to my mother and father, whose guidance and great teachings made me the man I am today. In between writing the last book and this one, I had a personal tragedy happen in my life.

My mother, who was my hero, passed away on March 14, 2014 at the tender age of 91. She was an amazing woman, and I know she would be proud of the words printed in this book. She gave me much wisdom and taught me to always be of the highest integrity. She always reminded me that when we pass, the only thing we have left is our good name.

I was humbled to be able to take care of her the last few years of her life as it changed me forever. When I was younger I did not appreciate the fact that I had such a loving mother whose sole purpose in life was to be there for me, no matter what, and to love me unconditionally. What an amazing person she was and I will miss terribly.

I try the best I can, with the talents God blessed me with and my ability to reach people and to hopefully change their lives, as I know they change mine.

We should all strive to be better and continually hone our craft however that looks like for you. We need to love more in this world. There is simply not enough of it to go around, so let us be cognizant of that which we require more of. Love is everything my dear readers, and I love the whole concept of love, as should you. It strengthens us while simultaneously making us weak in the knees. It is empowering and debilitating all at the same time.

Please be aware of each other as we are all we've got. *We* is better than *I* because together we can conquer all and stamp out evil. Together we are a team and that beats the heck out of anything else, because if you are not a team with each other, then you are, "I, ALONE!"

I want to thank some of my dear friends who have supported and encouraged me to never quit; and when I thought I was crazy, they all agreed with me; but they still loved me and told me to push on.

Thank you--Fraser S., Peter B., Debra P., Lowie, V.D., Kimmer B., Bon Bon and Raymond and Janie B. Also, a big thanks goes out to my fine staff that puts up with my madness each and every day, and who are always there for me as well: Alicia G., Arlena H., Robert S., David S. and Ioannis and Wanda O.

Your partner in success,
Aristides "Ari" Priakos

See other works at:

www.masterofseven.com

www.ingramcontent.com/pod-product-compliance
Lightning Source LLC
Chambersburg PA
CBHW052210090526
44584CB00016BA/2044